What Others Are Saying about

ABS of FAITH

Ours seems to be a day of strong bodies and flabby souls. Our culture puts great importance on physical exercise, but too many Christians are passive with respect to strengthening their spiritual muscles. At a time when so many self-help books seem to reduce spiritual growth to a half-dozen easy steps, Dan O'Deens makes a strong case for the necessity of spiritual discipline, forming habits that will result in spiritual fitness. As he states, spiritual fitness is not automatic; it takes time and effort. The purpose of this book is not merely to inform the reader; it is to help form him into the person God intends him to be.

Tom Julien, author of *Antioch Revisited, Reuniting The Church With Her Mission*

In *ABS of Faith*, Dan does a good job of touching on a very important issue, spiritual discipline, in a society that wants instant, easy, results. His writing is concise, practical, and positive. It's as though Dan, your "spiritual coach," is standing beside you reminding you that discipline and the work of the Holy Spirit is the key to growth in Christ-likeness. I recommend this book to those who want a practical guide for their spiritual journey.

Jeffrey A. Gill, D.Min., Dean, School of Ministries Studies, Grace Theological Seminary

A poignant reminder of the importance and power of living in community with other members of the body and the rightful place that God's Word should have in our lives. This book is a wakeup call for those who foolishly think that the

Christian life is to be lived privately; it is intensely personal but never meant to be private. We are created to live in biblical community, where a passion for knowing Christ is fueled by a love for His Word.

E. Scott Feather, Dean of the Chapel and Global Ministries, Grace College

I've had the honor not only of reading this book, but also *living it out* with Dan as his ABS partner for several years. I can tell you that my *ABS of Faith* have been stretched, strengthened, and made stronger through the principles and truths found in this book.

Mike Silliman, Church Planter/Pastor of Elk Creek Church

When I was young my abs were a true-six pack. I traded the six-pack in for a keg in more recent days, as I am no longer as concerned for physical conditioning as I am in spiritual. I have been exercising most of the core principles shared in this book for almost 20 years and I have to say it works. If your spiritual conditioning is at all important to you, I highly recommend the principles shared in this book.

Neil Cole, author of *Organic Church, Growing Faith Where Life Happens*

We can't be passive if we want to live in an abiding relationship with Jesus. It takes work. In *ABS of Faith*, Dan O'Deens writes about accountability, Bible study, and Scripture memorization; and we all need to grow in these three key disciplines of the Christian life*!*

Vince Antonucci, author of *I Became a Christian and All I Got Was This Lousy T-Shirt*

Failure to be disciplined in our Christian life leads to spiritual frailty and failings. Scripture reminds us that we must be disciplined if we are to achieve the purposes of godliness. Thankfully, in this important work Dan O'Deens presents a model that helps us find such discipline in our life. I know Dan to be one of the most gifted church planters I have ever met. He and his wife Gay moved to Pennsylvania to start a new church without any other people in their fledgling venture. But with God's provision in only a few short years they had planted a new and reproducing church that has helped transform their community and world. I often wondered in amazement at how Dan could attempt such a bold venture for God's glory. Now I know the secret…a deep faith and trust in the person of God…and a disciplined method of spiritual living that allowed that faith to germinate and grow. I praise God for their testimony and urge you to read this book! May you find here just the supplement you need for your own spiritual development. I know you will!

Tim Boal, Executive Director; GO2 Church Planting

As a leader in a local church, Dan has aggressively engaged the work of finding strategies both to reach and to effectively develop the people he reaches. In his book, Dan presents the successful spiritual habits he used in his ministry. This book could be a great tool to help church leaders develop the people they are reaching.

Brad Powell, Senior Pastor of NorthRidge Church and Author of *Change Your Church for Good, The Art of Sacred Cow Tipping*

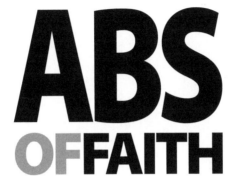

ABS OFFAITH

Dan O'Deens

ABS
OFFAITH

Dan O'Deens

BMH
www.bmhbooks.com
Winona Lake, IN 46590

ABS of Faith, Undergirded by Prayer
Helping Believers Gain Spiritual Muscle

Copyright ©2008 by Dan O'Deens
ISBN: 978-0-88469-310-9
RELIGION / Christian Life / Spiritual Growth

Published by BMH Books
BMH Books, P.O. Box 544, Winona Lake, IN 46590 USA
www.bmhbooks.com

The S.H.A.P.E. material on page 96 is adapted from Rick Warren, *The Purpose Driven Church* (Grand Rapids: Zondervan, 1995), p. 350. Used by Permission.

Printed in the United States of America

Dedication

To Gay

Life on this planet is worthwhile with you by my side. It is a joy to grow together with you. Thanks for balance and for pursuing spiritual fitness together with our kids and me. I love you!

To Mike

You have been an incredible friend and ABS Partner. I would trust my life with you. You are to me what Jonathan and Nathan were to King David. You lift me up and pick me up; you hear me out and you understand me when I struggle. You help set my feet back on solid ground and lift my eyes back to the ONE who makes the difference. I look forward to our get-togethers each week at Dunkin' Donuts and Starbucks!

To Gateway Church

Thanks for being a practice and playing field. Thanks for allowing me to make 1,000 mistakes so that together we could experience 100 successes. It is a joy to serve our great God together with you! I am so glad I am on your team!

To God

Thanks for grace and truth. Thanks too for allowing life to be a journey. Thanks for the struggles and the victories. Thanks for the promise that You will complete in me what You have begun. I love You with my life!

Special thanks to Roger Palms who did the tedious work of taking my thoughts, organizing them, and making them readable.

A very special thank you to Terry White and Jesse Deloe at BMH Books. They believed this was a worthy book that could be an asset to the body of Christ. Thanks for believing.

Contents

*This exercise program must be worked on
regularly and with balance.*

Preface

Everyone wants abs of steel. Washboard abs! Nothing wrong with that; I wouldn't mind a six-pack myself! But that is external and God is more interested in what is on the inside than what appears on the outside. So, what does it take to have ABS of Faith? Wouldn't it be great to have a person in your life who will provide a healthy Accountability structure for your life? Wouldn't it be great if you understood the Bible as God wrote it to help you map out your life to bring honor and glory to Him? Wouldn't it be great if you could memorize Scripture so you could resist the enemy at will? All undergirded with prayer so you can withstand the hard blows from the enemy? We need to ask God to strengthen us in the "inner man,"—*not a brute strength but a glorious inner strength* (Eph. 3:16, TM).

Another name for the inner man could be the word "guts." It takes guts to stand firm in our faith. When the flow of life is going south, it takes strength and stamina to go north. God doesn't want us to grow strong and develop abs of *steel*, but ABS of *Faith*. This book will help to develop in you the habits, disciplines, and skills that will make this possible in your life.

My prayer for you is found in 1Timothy 4:7 (NLT). Paul tells us to: *Spend your time and energy in training yourself for spiritual fitness.* There is no need for any of us to be spiritually unhealthy. This book not only tells us what we should be doing, but it also provides the "how to" and the resources that will equip us to be fully devoted followers of Christ. We can move from simply being hearers of the Word to being doers of the Word as well. Building spiritual abs is spiritual exercise.

Dan O'Deens

Part One

thePROCESS

…Spend your time and energy in training yourself for spiritual fitness

(1 Timothy 4:7 NLT)

Chapter 1

A Focus on Spiritual Maturity

When I was 20 years old and playing soccer for my university, I was in shape. Twenty-five years later, my passion for the game remains strong. But just because I was once in shape does not mean I can rely on that strength from years back. I have to keep working at building that strength. I may not have the legs I used to have, but my mind is still sharp. I know the game and stay in shape so I can use tools other than young legs. To stay physically fit, I need to develop some basic habits. That's true in the Christian life as well. The Bible says: Discipline yourself for the purpose of godliness (1Tim. 4:7 NASB). It takes discipline.

Let's focus on the exercises that all Christians need in order to build up their spiritual strength so they can grow to maturity. Here is a program that will equip believers with the skills needed to begin these spiritual abs-building habits. These tools will help make these exercises a daily routine. In the unity of common faith and the knowledge of the Son of God, we arrive at real maturity, the measure of development which is meant by the fullness of Christ (Eph. 4:13 Phillips). Spiritual maturity can be defined in one phrase: Spiritual maturity is being like Christ.

This has been God's goal for us all along. God knew what He was doing from the very beginning. He decided from the outset to shape the lives of those who love Him along the same lines as the life of his Son (Rom. 8:29, TM). From the very beginning of time, back in the Garden of Eden when God made man, He said, "Let us make man in our image." From the very beginning God has said, "I want to make man like Myself, not to be gods, but to be godly." We are not intended to be sovereign like God but to possess the character of God.

Unfortunately, as a result of sin, that image was marred. God's original design of making man in His own image was no longer an image of perfection. Adam was made in the image of God, but he sinned and was no longer perfect. God would have to put a plan into place that would restore man to that original state. It would be a plan that would make man complete or whole again.

The word "mature" carries the idea of perfect or complete. Without Jesus, God's Son, coming to this earth and becoming a man so He could die on a cross to pay the penalty for our sin, none of us could be reconciled to God and brought back to that original state.

Becoming spiritually mature is like the training of an athlete. Athletes get up every morning and go to the gym. They discipline their schedule. They sweat and work out. They "work it 'til it hurts." An athlete does not wake up one morning and look in the mirror and stare at six-pack abs. Committed athletes work hard to get abs of steel. Although it would be nice to stare at a six-pack, I would far rather work on something that is eternal. Our challenge is to develop ABS of Faith! Instant ABS of Faith are not going to happen. Here are some important facts about spiritual maturity.

It's Not Automatic

A person can be a Christian and never grow up spiritually. Scripture teaches, You have been Christians for a long time now, and you ought to be teaching others Instead you need someone to teach you (Heb. 5:12 NLT). When a person is still living on spiritual milk, it shows. He isn't very far along in the Christian life. He's still a baby Christian. The author of Hebrews is letting us know that spiritual abs-building is not automatic. It takes time and effort. We have to work it!

It's a Process

"Learn to be mature," we are told. The Bible says we should continue to grow in the grace and knowledge of our Lord and Savior Jesus Christ (2 Peter 3:18). That indicates a process. It's not instantaneous. There is no shortcut to spiritual growth. There is no pill we can take that makes us spiritually mature. Rather, the Bible says it's a continual process. We have to learn to be mature and there are some skills we can learn that will help us grow and build ABS of Faith.

It Takes Discipline

Discipline is the main thing. When an athlete begins to struggle, he goes back to the main thing. He must remember always to keep the main thing the main thing. This is the main thing if we want to develop ABS of Faith: …Spend your time and energy in training yourself for spiritual fitness (1 Tim. 4:7 NLT). Physical fitness is not automatic. Neither is spiritual fitness. It takes time and effort. That process is true for the new athlete in Christ just as it is for an older athlete.

The word discipline refers to a process or a journey. Spiritually, we call that process discipleship because the two go together. The Bible teaches that a mature believer is a disciple. The Bible teaches that I cannot be a disciple without being disciplined. The Bible also teaches that the more disciplined I become, the more God can begin to use me. The more I am disciplined in the faith, the more ready I am to be put on God's playing field.

What are the habits necessary to build ABS of Faith? Rick Warren's description of habit catches my attention. He defines habit as "a continual, often unconscious inclination to do a certain activity, acquired through frequent repetition."

The fact is, all of us are simply bundles of habits. We are the sum total of our habits. If I were to look at some other person's life, most of the things that person does, he does by habit—he wakes up, brushes his teeth, shaves, eats breakfast, drives to work, drives home from work, has dinner, reads the newspaper, watches some television and goes to bed. We are all creatures of habit.

If we desire to become spiritually mature or complete then we have to develop the habits that will move us toward that goal. I need to hang out with the One who can produce those habits in me. I have to "abide with Him," Jesus told us. If I hang with Jesus, He reproduces His character in me. This is one area that is an exciting contrast to abs of steel. I cannot truly develop ABS of Faith on my own. Christ produces them in me. I submit to a different set of daily disciplines and perform my schedule of training in God's gym, not Gold's gym. The key to success in developing ABS of Faith starts in the mind. In fact, it comes from a renewing of our minds. That simply means that I have to get rid of the old habits and develop some new ones.

Very few people are capable of working out by themselves and achieving rewarding results. We all need a workout partner. This partner is our "ABS partner" or our "ABS group."

Chapter 2

What Is an ABS Partner or Group?

Whated I go to the gym to lift weights I seek out a personal trainer. I want to hang with someone who has been there and knows what he or she is talking about. That person provides leadership in specific areas where I need special attention. A personal trainer holds me accountable not only to my goals but also to the basic exercise regimens that are necessary to provide balance. In the same way, an ABS partner or group is a person or several persons who want to assist me on my journey to attain my desired spiritual goals.

An ABS partner or group is a coaching and training system. Neil Cole, in *Raising Leaders for the Harvest*, says, "In professional baseball we see the best example: minor league and major league. The purpose of the minor league is to prepare potential athletes in the basic skills that will be needed to perform at the highest level. When a player shows he has developed these skills, he moves from single-A ball to double-A ball and then to triple-A ball. He is then ready for the majors."[1]

We may never have the opportunity to play in the majors, but every believer who commits to the development of ABS of Faith gets to play at an even higher level. We play for the glory of God. Just as the baseball system requires a good farm system

---

[1] Robert E. Logan and Neil Cole, *Raising Leaders for the Harvest*. (St. Charles, Ill.: ChurchSmart Resources), Audiocassette, tape 2.

to keep it strong, God's team also needs a system to establish healthy and strong players for God's playing field.

ABS of Faith is a spiritual fitness program that allows for the natural development and reproduction of true disciples of Christ. If we follow the example of Christ, the system gets the job done. The system must not be merely academic or informational, but transformational.

Everyone wants to play for the top team but not many are willing to pay the price to get there. Everyone wants the perks; few want to pay the price of discipline and training. The great news about God's team is that there are no cuts or salary caps. We can be on the team but we need to be willing to pay the price.

To see as many people as possible develop ABS of Faith and become mature disciples, we need to see what that picture of success looks like. If we organize the teams that are in development and put them onto the playing field without defining what success is, it will be like playing soccer without any goals.

To develop ABS of Faith we must understand the difference between efficiency and effectiveness. At first glance they look very similar, but the results of efficiency and effectiveness are different. Efficiency results from doing things right. Managers are people who do things right. But that is not enough. Effectiveness results not merely from doing things right but from doing the right things. Trainers and mentors are people who do the right things. They show that success in the Christian life is about doing the right things. The right thing is to develop ABS of Faith.[2]

A good coach, no matter what the sport, always teaches the fundamentals. As the team develops and still shows signs of struggle, the coach returns to the basics. A spiritually mature person, having a proper foundation, is one who spends time in

[2] Ideas from Warren Bennis and Burt Nanus: "Leaders: Strategies for Taking Charge." *Harper Business,* 1985, 1997, p. 20.

God's Word—reading it, memorizing it, and meditating on it. He has a life undergirded with prayer. These are basic.

How are we able to judge the success of our future leaders, the next generation of trainers and coaches? The success of spiritual athletes depends on the strength of their spiritual foundation.

Three Foundational Characteristics

Consider three foundational characteristics found in God's Word.

Faithfulness

Well done, good and faithful servant...Come and share your master's happiness (Matt.25:21; 1 Cor. 4:2).

Fruitfulness

My Father is glorified by this, that you bear much fruit, and so prove to be my disciples (John 15:8 NASB).

Finishing Well

I have fought the good fight, I have finished the course, I have kept the faith (2 Tim. 4:7 NASB).

If we are going to build a training foundation, then our systems have to be in line with God's plan. We have to recruit in God's playing field, and that field is called the harvest. We have to identify people who want to develop their ABS of Faith and begin to nurture those "out of shape" bodies into fully mature, Christ-like specimens.

For Every Believer

ABS groups are for every believer, and even for pre-believers who are willing to commit themselves to the process. The Great Commission is to all believers and it is all-encompassing. The goal is to make disciples, and we do that by following the threefold strategy that God gives us in that commission.

By going!

This is simply being obedient to share our faith with nonbelievers. This is evangelism.

By baptizing!

This is simply helping a new believer to make a public proclamation that he is now to be identified under a new management structure. He is now sold out to being a God the Father, God the Son, and God the Holy Spirit kind of person.

By teaching!

Teach them to observe all that God has commanded. That is discipleship. The most effective way to teach people is to develop healthy, authentic relationships with them. No agenda is necessary; curriculum is not needed. Living life in biblical community happens as life unfolds and dishes out victories and defeats and ups and downs.

Defining an ABS Partner or Group

An ABS of Faith partner or group provides an opportunity to connect people to God, to each other, and to their world. ABS groups work best with two or three people. Everyone who plays on God's team should have a minimum of one ABS partner. Every believer in Christ should have a mentor, someone to whom he or she looks for spiritual coaching. Equally, each believer should be training a new disciple. It is possible to be part of two groups at the same time.

The value of three persons is practical. With only two people it is easier to bypass the goals of the group. We feel freer to go off on tangents that are not part of the fitness routine needed to stay in shape spiritually. Three people work better for accountability. Even the Godhead exists in a community of three.

This structure builds the important dynamics that are essential to the making of a spiritually fit disciple of Christ.

Certain key elements should be recognized and practiced each week in a group.

Community

A person standing alone can be attacked and defeated, but two can stand back-to-back and conquer. Three are even better, for a triple-braided cord is not easily broken (Eccl. 4:12 NLT).

Everyone needs to be in community. We were made for community. We were created for community. We need Christ and we need others in our lives. This small community should be made up of brothers or sisters of the same gender who love each other enough to speak into each others' lives, not only words of encouragement but also words of rebuke that will set us on the right path. When I choose to live my life in biblical community with others I am able to live authentically before my Lord and my peers. This group will love me even when I fail, and if I fall they will be there to pick me up. We all need community.

Accountability

Obey your spiritual leaders and do what they say. Their work is to watch over your souls, and they know they are accountable to God. Give them reason to do this joyfully and not with sorrow. That would certainly not be for your benefit (Heb. 13:17 NLT).

Accountability is a word that is often over-used and way too often not understood. The essence of accountability is honesty, and you alone are the only one who can hold yourself accountable. This is an issue of character. You will have to trust those whom you invite into your community to ask you the tough questions that probe the motives of your heart and follow the shadows of your footsteps as you walk through the pages of your life. When your feet or your mind wander into darkness, you must resist the urge to live in a lifestyle of inauthentic relationship with your Father in heaven and your brothers or sisters in Christ. You must tell the truth and trust your biblical community to help you get back onto the pathway of light.

Confidentiality

Don't be so naive and self-confident. You're not exempt. You could fall flat on your face as easily as anyone else. Forget about self-confidence; it's useless. Cultivate God-confidence. *"He who guards his mouth and his tongue keeps himself from calamity"* (Prov. 21:23 NIV).

While confidentiality is all about holding a confidence, it is not merely the ability to hold a secret. Sometimes the best way to help a person is to bring the appropriate people into the circle of community so that the person can regain spiritual fitness. It is true that the success of the group depends on the ability for sensitive information to stay in this group. But, if I love someone deeply enough to share the struggles I am going through, then I must equally trust that person to take that information and do what is best for me. The old phrase, "What happens in Vegas stays in Vegas" is not what God had in mind. God did not come to condemn the world. He came to save the world. That includes all of us. He came not for the healthy, but for the sick, therefore you can place your full confidence in Him and in those who choose to follow Him.

Flexibility

For where two are three have gathered in my name, there I am in their midst (Matt. 18:20 NASB).

Flexibility is a critical word, because too often we follow the fallacious tendency to think "biblical community" happens only in a building that some call church. The church is bigger than a building or a program. The church is God's people! The point is that ABS groups can meet all over the community. They can meet in the local diner, at St. Arbucks. (Some might know it better as Starbucks, but it is amazing how many spiritual conversations and spiritual fitness habits have been conducted over a great cup of java!) Sometimes the phone is good enough. Mike (my ABS partner) and I often call each other. He might be in Boston and I in California. We take advantage of the high-tech world in which we live.

Reproducibility

You have heard me teach many things that have been confirmed by many reliable witnesses. Teach these great truths to trustworthy people who are able to pass them on to others (2 Tim. 2:2 NLT).

As we grow spiritually, we call that maturity. At the very basic level of maturity one is recognized as able to reproduce. As children move through the stages of life development and pass those hard years of puberty and move into early stages of adulthood, they are able to reproduce. The same should be true spiritually, with one difference. Spiritual maturity is not measured by the number of spiritual children, but the number of grandchildren and even great-grandchildren. The mark of a person who is becoming spiritually fit is seen in the number of people he or she leads to the Lord and then helps them to grow in their relationship with the Lord so they too will be able to lead their family, friends, coworkers and, neighbors to the Lord.

Chapter 3

The Formation of an ABS Group

ABS groups can be churches within a church. They are microcosms of the larger body of Christ. A mi·cro·cosm is simply "a diminutive, (small) representative system analogous to a larger system in composition, development, or configuration" www.nsc.org/ehc/glossar1.htm. These groups are led by the same overseer of the universal church, the local church, or larger corporate church. We know that person as Jesus Christ. The Spirit of God is our teacher. Literally the Spirit of God is the Spirit of Jesus. He is evidenced in both the written Word—the very pages of Scripture—and the Living Word, who lives within the hearts of believers. As we read from the text, as we meditate on the text, as we memorize the text and even as we discuss the text, He reveals meaning and enlightens us to its truth.

The author of the text does not merely live on the pages of Scripture. He is living and active in the believer's life as well. We know that He can convict us of sin, that He can guide our thoughts, sometimes He even reveals himself in mystical ways that seem to defy conservative theology. (God cannot be contained in a box.) The point is that God speaks to us through the pages of Scripture and sometimes He speaks to us through a friend, a pastor, a mentor and maybe even a still, small voice. The real question is, "are we listening? And, if He is speaking are we ready to follow His lead and obey what He is telling us to do?

We know from Scripture that: *Two are better off than one ... If one of them falls down, the other can help him up. But if someone is alone and falls, it's just too bad, because there is no one to help him ... Two people can resist an attack that would defeat one person alone. A rope made of three cords is hard to break* (Ecclesiastes 4:9–10, 12 GN). And, the Bible shows us, *People learn from one another just as iron sharpens iron* (Proverbs 27:17 GN).

The writer of Hebrews tells us that the need is ongoing, *You must warn each other every day, as long as it is called "today," so that none of you will be deceived by sin and hardened against God* (Hebrews 3:13 NLT).

We should genuinely care about one another to the point of action. When a brother falls we should lift him up. When a friend's burden is heavy we should offer a hand to make his burden lighter. *Brothers, if someone is caught in a sin, you who are spiritual should restore him gently. But watch yourself, or you also may be tempted. Carry each other's burdens, and in this way you will fulfill the law of Christ* (Galatians 6:1–2).

ABS groups are formed organically and relationally. These groups are not intended to be the church but to function similarly, a microcosm of the church. These groups could be the church, but are not designed intentionally to be the church. The formation of these groups is to allow spiritual formation to multiply exponentially, limited only by the Holy Spirit. There is no governing authority or system holding it back. Neil Cole, in *The Organic Church*, says,

> We want to lower the bar of how church is done and raise the bar of what it means to be a disciple. Church is not a once a week service. The organic or simple church, more than any other, is best prepared to saturate a region because it is informal, relational and mobile. It also reproduces faster and spreads further.[1]

[1] Neil Cole, *Organic Church: Growing Faith Where Life Happens* (San Francisco: Jossey-Bass, 2005) 26-27.

ABS groups can be started quickly and are relationally based. ABS groups do not require big budgets, because the teacher is the Spirit of God and the groups do not require church structures (buildings). They are mobile and can meet anywhere. They are smaller realities of the local church and are able to stand up in the face of persecution. They are difficult to break up.

These groups could be seen as 'seed' for future local church plants that wish to come together for a larger corporate celebration. But large group celebration is neither their mission nor their aim. The heart of an ABS group is to: *Spend your time and energy in training yourself for spiritual fitness* (1 Tim.4:7 NLT).

How Do ABS Groups Work?

1. Groups meet once a week for approximately one hour. They can meet almost anywhere. One hour is plenty of time to accomplish the needed elements, but the meeting can certainly go longer, depending on the available time and flexibility of its members.

2. They are groups of only two or three people. A fourth person should be considered as the first person beginning the next group. Multiplication should be imminent.

3. The need for honesty and transparency during the confession of sin requires that the group not be coed. Confession to God is necessary for forgiveness. Confession to other men or to other women in the group is necessary for freedom.

4. There is no set curriculum. Each group can determine what it desires to work through. In the Appendix to this chapter, there are several ideas that might work for the group. The key to any ABS Group is strict adherence to the Word of God. And let the peace that comes from Christ rule in your hearts. For as members of one body you are all called to live in peace (Colossians 3:15 NLT). We always allow the Holy Spirit to be our guide.

5. There is no appointed leader. Most groups find that the one who starts the group ends up being the leader. That person may facilitate the group but should not take charge. The best groups are the ones that offer shared leadership.

6. People in the group ask specific accountability questions. The first thing the members do when they meet together is to ask one another accountability questions. The atmosphere must one of confidentiality, honesty, and mutual accountability. The purpose of these questions is for confession of sin and relational restoration to occur between each member and God and their fellow man.

7. Each member of the group will read the assigned Scripture passage, commit to memory the verse for the week, and commit to pray for himself and the other members of the group.

Why Are ABS Groups Important?

1. They allow any person at any level to lead. There is no need to report to the pastor. These groups will learn they can find their strength in the One who is truly capable of giving it.

2. As the ABS groups meet, there is one accountability question that is primary: "Have you been a faithful, verbal testimony this week concerning your relationship with the Lord Jesus Christ?" Evangelism for every believer is not optional. If we do not share our faith, we cannot be true disciples of Christ.

3. ABS groups allow the mighty power of the Holy Spirit to do "God Stuff" in the lives of each member. The people of God will be reunited with genuine strength. I ask him to strengthen you by his Spirit—not a brute strength but a glorious inner strength (Ephesians 3:16 MSG).

4. ABS groups are the future of an effective small-group ministry. As ABS groups multiply, these small groups can

get together for larger group experiences such as socials, outreach parties, worship gatherings, and communion. These small groups can then be part of the great body of Christ in a larger assembly or local church.

5. The natural result of people who have met with God is they look like they have met with God. When Moses came down from the mountain, the people knew he had been with God. The best-prepared minister or servant in the church is not the one who has only prepared the best curriculum, but the one who has prepared his heart.

Are ABS Groups Easy to Start and Easy to Control?

1. To start an ABS group, find another person or persons (no more than three) whom you trust. This will work with either believers or unbelievers so long as the people in the group will commit to doing the work. The end result will be salvation or personal spiritual growth, and hopefully, both.

2. The groups are easy to control because we do not seek to control them. Each group chooses its own Scripture reading plan and memory verses. They move at their own pace. They select the location where they will regularly meet. There is plenty of flexibility concerning the meeting location, but it is essential to communicate so the members of the group know where and when they are to meet. This eliminates any unnecessary confusion.

3. A person should commit to one ABS group primarily. It is possible for mature believers to be involved in more than one if their motive is to invest in more than two other people at one period of time. The goal, however, is multiplication. Being a part of more than two groups at a time will result in an informational maintenance oriented system that will be less relational and will jeopardize the transformational reproducing model that you are trying to

foster. Relationship is the key. Focus on a few and attempt to multiply your ABS groups by allowing them to multiply organically.

How Do We Start a Group?

1. Each group should be formed more by natural affinity than by organizational structure.

2. Look for others who are interested in Christ and want to grow in relationship with Him. Approach someone and ask, "Would you be interested in starting an ABS group with me?" This question will naturally raise the question, "What is an ABS group?" You are now prepared to inform them.

3. Keep in mind that these groups should be multiplying groups. As you find a partner, why not ask an unsaved or newer believer to join the group? The critical reality of group formation is that each person takes seriously the pursuit of genuinely seeking a personal relationship with Jesus and finding out whether a relationship with Jesus is worth giving one's life to. As long as each member is committed to reading the Scriptures and memorizing the verses that each group chooses and is equally committed to authentic relationship with Jesus and the other group members, the result will be either new birth or an exodus of the one who is not really interested in searching out a personal relationship with God. Let the Spirit of God be your guide and He will make it clear when you should multiply your group.

What Do People Do in Their ABS Group?

Accountability

Every group begins with the accountability questions. These questions will stimulate interaction. We need to create a safe, authentic place that provides men and women with the ability to interact in Spirit-led conversations. This happens only when there is a genuine trust within the groups. That trust is borne out of authentic relationships.

Prayer

Prayer is as vital to the spiritual life of a Christian as air is to our physical life. The power and strength of anything that has spiritual substance is always undergirded with prayer. This prayer time should not be regimented but should happen naturally and spontaneously as a result of hearing the needs that are shared in the group.

Scripture memorization

Each person should be able to quote the Scripture memorization for the week.

Discussion

The group will discuss the Bible reading. Don't let this discussion turn into a pooling of ignorance. Group members should be men and women driven to discover what the Holy Spirit is teaching through the Bible. When someone doesn't know the answer to a question, seek the answer until you see it in the pages of Scripture. The resources included in the text and the additional resources at the end of the book are tools that will help you find the answers to biblical questions.

A Get-Started Check List

☐ Select two potential disciples (of the same gender) who can begin meeting weekly. Remember, there is no leader but nothing happens without someone taking initiative. You might be asked to join a group, but you could be a catalyst for God's reproductive system. Why not seek out another person today?

☐ Structure group(s) in such a way as not to be leader-dependent.

☐ Integrate accountability into the group(s) for confession of sin and for Bible reading and Scripture memorization.

☐ Group members read through the selected Scripture throughout the week.

☐ Keep evangelism in the minds of each group member by adding new members who are "pre-Christians."

☐ Groups multiply spontaneously when a fourth person is added.

Accountability Questions for Spiritual Fitness

The Tough Questions
When the going gets tough, the tough get going.

1. Have you been keeping up with your Bible reading and prayer?

2. Have you been a verbal and living testimony this week concerning your relationship to Jesus Christ?

3. How much time have you spent with your family?

4. Are you harboring resentment toward someone whom you need to forgive?

5. Have you offended anyone, either by your actions or words? How and when will you make it right?

6. Have you lost control of your temper?

7. Have you given in to a personal addiction?

8. Are you maintaining a healthy lifestyle (sleep, exercise, diet, outlets for stress)?

9. Have you been in a compromising situation with a member of the opposite sex or been exposed to any sexually explicit material (movies, Internet, magazines, or books)?

10. Have you been honest in all your dealings?

11. Are you making progress in your personal goals?

12. Is your life showing the characteristics of the fruit of the Spirit, Galatians 5:22-23? Is your thought-life in line with Philippians 4:8?

13. Come up with your own personalized question.

14. Have you just lied to me about any of these questions?

Carry each other's burdens, and in this way you will fulfill the law of Christ (Galatians 6:2).

Accountability Questions for Personal Purity

Use this worksheet to develop a personal question tailored to your own unique temptations (#13–Tough Questions).

1 In what general area of your life not already covered by the questions do you struggle most consistently (i.e., thought life, time management, communication, confrontation)?

2 In that general area, what issue is the most repetitive and specific behavioral problem?

3 Draft a question that addresses your specific area of weakness.

4 Evaluate your question's first draft by the following criteria:

- Does it directly address a specific behavioral weakness?
- Does it specifically hold you accountable for the past week?
- Is it specific? Concise? Memorable? A measurable behavior?

5 Rewrite the question with any needed corrections and transcribe it in legible form on the Accountability Questions for Personal Integrity as the thirteenth question.

Strategic Prayer Focus

Each person is to identify at least two people to pray for once every week, so all are praying for their salvation weekly. Check the box next to each name when they accept Christ as their Savior.

1. Pray that God draws them to Himself as only He can (John 6:44).

2. Pray that they will seek to know God (Acts 17:27).

3. Pray that they believe the word of God (1 Thessalonians 2:13).

4. Pray that Satan is kept from blinding them to the truth (2 Corinthians 4:4; 2 Timothy 2:25–26).

5. Ask the Holy Spirit to convict them of sin and their need for Christ's redemption (John 16:8–13).

6. Ask God to send someone who will share the gospel with them (Matthew 9:37–38).

7. Pray that God would give you the opportunity, the courage, and the right words to share the truth with them (Colossians 4:3–6; Ephesians 6:19–20).

8. Pray that they turn from their sin (Acts 17:30-31).

9. Pray that they would put all their trust in Christ (John 1:12, 5:24).

10. Pray that they make Christ the Lord of their life (Romans 10:9–10).

11. Ask that they take root and grow in faith (Colossians 2:6–7).

Chapter 4

What About Accountability?

My Story – A Pastor and Pornography

When I was four years old I asked Jesus to come into my life. I knew at a very early age that hell was not a place where I wanted to go. My parents enrolled me in a Christian school, and when I was in ninth grade, I knew the Lord wanted me to become a pastor. I went to Word of Life Bible Institute, Philadelphia College of the Bible, and Grace Theological Seminary. I lived in Israel for half a year, and then took my first youth pastorate. Ten years later I became a church planter and now I am the founding and senior pastor of a growing church.

That sounds good, but not when I color between the lines. After I was in Israel, I decided to take an excursion on my flight home and arranged to backpack through Europe for a month. I got off the plane in Belgium only to find that my backpack did not get off, so I rearranged my plans and decided to go north first. I have a Jewish background and thought it would be good to see Anne Frank's house. It was great! I did not realize that I would be traveling through one of the world's darkest cities—Amsterdam. It was only by God's grace that I walked out of that city a virgin.

What I experienced in that city haunted me and my ministry for the next 15 years. What I allowed my eyes to see on that trip led me into an addiction to pornography.

I fought it and wrestled with it. I would win...but then I would lose. My life was a constant frustration. I found myself teaching that the things we allow to come into our minds will never be released. Those pictures would always be there as a constant struggle. I wanted to be released; I wanted freedom. I just could not find it!

Then God broke me! It was about 1999, while at a conference with a group of men and women, that the Holy Spirit made me so sick of my sin, I decided to set it free. I shared my story with this group. That was only the beginning of the story. The freedom would not come until the end of the year. As I enlisted myself in God's plan for pure freedom, I was exposed to the Word of God that revealed a God who longed to release me from the bondage of sin. He wanted me to have a healthy and authentic relationship with Him. I began to empty me of me and all the other stuff that was holding me captive, and I replaced it with something far better—an authentic relationship with Jesus. I began to drink from the deep well of living water. Soon the desire for pornography was replaced by a relationship with Jesus.

Although I became a child of God at a very young age, my conception of God was more of an angry Father who carried a large bat around, just waiting for me to mess up. And when I did, I graciously took my licking because I felt I deserved it.

That was a misunderstanding of the grace of God. Grace is God's giving me exactly what I need the most and what I deserve the least. I did not need a beating; I needed God's grace in my life. For the first time I realized that God desired a personal relationship with me for who I am and not for what I had done or might do again. I was stunned to read the wonderful Scripture, *The Word became flesh and made his dwelling among us. We have seen his glory, the glory of the One and Only, who came from the Father, full of grace and truth* (John 1:14). Literally that means grace upon grace! He cannot be emptied of grace. It keeps on coming. His grace is not dependent on my ability to remain sinless. What I learned was freeing. I was now enjoying a relationship with a God who loved me for who I am and not for what I did or might still struggle with.

There is a very interesting correlation between intimacy and closed doors. Jesus was telling me to go into my room and close the door. He wanted me to go where no one else was looking and get alone with Him. I was now able to find myself experiencing a new level of intimacy with my creator—my Savior. As I found myself connected to the Vine, abiding with the Vine—the Word—Jesus, the most amazing thing happened. My mind began to be cleansed. I thought I would always have those images in my mind. Jesus removed them. I was able to see clearly and cleanly! This freedom lasts as long as I am intimately connected to, and abiding in, the Word.

Looking Up to Someone

Almost everyone is looking up to someone, and someone may be looking up to you. We cannot go through life and escape the watchful eye of people around us. As we journey through life most of us want to leave a legacy of significance. We want to have a lasting impact on the people who live around us.

Mentoring is a buzzword of our day. Chambers of Commerce and local businesses are working to pair budding leaders with current leaders. This is not just a business maneuver; it is a biblical principle as well. The apostle Paul said to young Timothy, his spiritual son, *So, my son, throw yourself into this work for Christ. Pass on what you heard from me—the whole congregation saying Amen!—to reliable leaders who are competent to teach others* (2 Tim. 2:1–2 MSG*)*.

If we are going to have the kind of impact on others that Paul was communicating to his student, we must recognize the implications of mentoring. Paul was not simply interested in training Timothy. He knew that for Timothy to grow, he, too, would have to invest himself into the life of another person. It is fair to say that we do not fully understand something until we can properly articulate it. What we learn from our "up" teacher, we must pass "down" to our students.

If we desire to invest our lives in others, we will need to give away our precious time and energy. Time spent with people is our greatest gift to them. If we are to make an impact that will last for eternity, we must invest our lives in what will last forever. Only two things will last forever. One is the Word of God. The other is people. People are eternal beings. We must invest ourselves into that person on whom God has placed such a high value.

In an age where outcomes have become increasingly important, where productivity determines the value of a person, it is important that we understand this principle. If we simply invest all our energy on goals and outcomes, we will miss the opportunity to invest in the one thing that will bring about the results we are striving to attain—other people.

Where Real Accountability Begins

This is where real accountability begins. We will answer to the Lord for what we have done with His Word and for how we have made an impact on those whom He created in His image. Accountability to God is both inescapable and inevitable. Matthew 12:35–36 tells us, *The good man brings good things out of the good stored up in him, and the evil man brings evil things out of the evil stored up in him. But I tell you that men will have to give account on the day of judgment for every careless word they have spoken.*

Romans 14:10–12 asks, *You, then, why do you judge your brother? Or why do you look down on your brother? For we will all stand before God's judgment seat. It is written: "As surely as I live," says the Lord, "every knee will bow before me; every tongue will confess to God." So then, each of us will give an account of himself to God.*

Every person will answer to God. We would do well to remember that. Most of us recognize that we will at least answer to God and therefore we might be willing to hold ourselves accountable to Him. But that is only the first step of accountability.

For Our Own Good

The second part of accountability is to recognize that God has placed spiritual leaders over us for our own good. 1 Corinthians 16:13–16, *Be on your guard; stand firm in the faith; be men of courage; be strong. Do everything in love. You know that the household of Stephanas were the first converts in Achaia, and they have devoted themselves to the service of the saints. I urge you, brothers, to submit to such as these and to everyone who joins in the work, and labors at it.*

Hebrews 13:17 states, *Obey your leaders and submit to their authority. They keep watch over you as men who must give an account. Obey them so that their work will be a joy, not a burden, for that would be of no advantage to you.*

We sometimes forget there are people who have given themselves to the study of God's Word so they will be able to point people in the right direction—God's direction. These men and women of God are gifts from God to us. We need to listen to them and give careful attention to their words of wisdom. We must obey them when that wisdom is the Word of Truth.

The World of "Me-ism"

We have identified the two "normal" forms of accountability, but there is another specific facet of accountability that we need to understand. We have built up personal defenses against it. We have bought into the world system of "me-ism" that is perhaps the most destructive tool of our enemy today. In that world we won't let anyone get close to us. If someone gets too close, there is too much risk involved—the risk of being found out for who we really are. The underlying problem, however, is really not "me-ism," but instead it's a lack of trust. We begin to believe we cannot trust anyone with the information or pain that is heavy on our hearts, causing severe physical and spiritual stress. Therefore we bear it alone and that leads to human failure and despair.

God did not create us this way.

Brothers, if someone is caught in a sin, you who are spiritual should restore him gently. But watch yourself, or you also may be tempted. Carry each other's burdens, and in this way you will fulfill the law of Christ. If anyone thinks he is something when he is nothing, he deceives himself. Each one should test his own actions. Then he can take pride in himself, without comparing himself to somebody else, for each one should carry his own load (Galatians 6:1–5).

We need each other.

Imagine a sea of people gathered *en masse*, filling an entire park to capacity. At the front there is a platform and a lectern. A speaker delivers a great message. It is compelling; it is challenging. The entire crowd has been overcome with a task larger than any one person could handle on his own. The speaker asks for a response. He calls for a show of hands as he asks, "Who is with me?"

Every individual in the crowd is now in this picture with a little "thought cloud" over his or her head, all saying the very same thing, "I will if someone else will. But, no one else is, so I won't."

Each individual must bear the personal weight of the challenge. Each person must raise his own hand and take responsibility for his own actions. Each person in the crowd wants the same thing. All want to accomplish the task, but the task is greater than they can handle as individuals. Now the entire crowd is raising their hands.

I do not know any person who does not wish to be free from sin. I do not know anyone who wishes to bear the heavy weight of his own sin. All of us are sinners. There is no one righteous, according to God's Word. We are all in the same boat. Each of us needs to understand both sides of responsibility. There is personal responsibility for sin. No one else thought what I thought; no one dragged me into that establishment in Amsterdam. I got there on my own. That is the first level of responsibility. With that level of responsibility comes personal confession. As I confess my sin to my Father, He has promised to cleanse me of any wrongdoing. I am forgiven at that level.

The second level is a bit more difficult, but it is necessary for full restoration. Here I confess before others. At this level of responsibility, I receive freedom in addition to forgiveness. The initial step is difficult because I feel I am the only one and am feeling the weight of my sin or my burden. I need to recognize that I am standing by a sea of fellow strugglers. We are here to help each other, not to tear each other apart. I need to know that people are more forgiving than I think. When I am transparent enough to take responsibility, people will come alongside to help me. That is not only our responsibility; it is a command from our Heavenly Father!

Accountability to one another is both helpful and healthy.

Love must be sincere. Hate what is evil; cling to what is good. Be devoted to one another in brotherly love. Honor one another above yourselves. Never be lacking in zeal, but keep your spiritual fervor, serving the Lord. Be joyful in hope, patient in affliction, faithful in prayer. Share with God's people who are in need. Practice hospitality.

Bless those who persecute you; bless and do not curse. Rejoice with those who rejoice; mourn with those who mourn. Live in harmony with one another. Do not be proud, but be willing to associate with people of low position. Do not be conceited.

Do not repay anyone evil for evil. Be careful to do what is right in the eyes of everybody. If it is possible, as far as it depends on you, live at peace with everyone. Do not take revenge, my friends, but leave room for God's wrath, for it is written: "It is mine to avenge; I will repay," says the Lord (Romans 12:9–19).

We all must wrestle to get rid of our pride. We have to let go of the lies that have held us captive to sin. Not only do we need God and spiritual leadership, but also we need each other. Our enemy wants to make us believe our brothers and sisters will hate us, will think less of us, if they know the truth about us. They might take away our ministry. They might rub our face in the bed of sin that we have laid. We are afraid of what they will say. We are afraid of the temporary consequences, and we buy into our adversary's greatest lie. Thus we never experience living in the freedom of Christ. We forfeit the abundant life by living an inauthentic life before God, others, and ourselves. We are in bondage and Satan has us right where he wants us.

If the church desires to be healthy, it must encourage the accountability of one to another. This accountability must lead to genuine forgiving of the one who asks for it. Loving accountability is the missing key to countless believers feeling as though they can never be fully restored to Jesus Christ. Repentance and confession to God gives us forgiveness. Repentance and confession to others gives us freedom. We need and want both. How can we be restored to the body of Christ fully when only the Head is willing to forgive? To be fully restored, the body must submit to the desires of the Head.

A trained athlete is marked by discipline. Athletes don't look at discipline as a bad thing. As we develop ABS of Faith and pursue spiritual maturity and completeness, we should embrace God's pattern of discipline. Discipline is not punishment; it is God's training field to scrape off the impurities that keep us from shining like gold. Biblical discipline always has restoration and fellowship as God's desire for us. Shouldn't it be our desire, too?

There are three practical advantages to holding ourselves accountable to God's spiritual regimen if we are going to play on God's playing field.

Recognizing Our Enemy

The first advantage of accountability is that it enables us to recognize who our enemy is. When we can identify the enemy we are less likely to fall into his trap. Our enemy is Satan, the one whom the Bible refers to as the "Father of Lies," the "Master of Deception," "the one who prowls around seeking whom he may devour." "Devour" is a strong word. Satan is not content merely to trip us up; he wants to take us out. Never underestimate the power of this enemy. For the moment, he is "the god of this age." He knows our greatest weakness and he will set traps for us at every possible intersection.

Pride only breeds quarrels,
but wisdom is found in those who take advice.
The teaching of the wise is a fountain of life,
turning a man from the snares of death.
He who ignores discipline comes to poverty and shame,
but whoever heeds correction is honored.
He who walks with the wise grows wise,
but a companion of fools suffers harm
(Prov. 13:10, 14, 18, 20).

He who listens to a life-giving rebuke
will be at home among the wise.
He who ignores discipline despises himself,
but whoever heeds correction gains understanding.
The fear of the LORD teaches a man wisdom,
and humility comes before honor
(Prov. 15:31-33).

When we follow the wisdom of a spiritual coach and hold ourselves accountable to him, the Bible says we are given a fountain of life instead of a life that leads to a "snare of death" (Prov. 14:27).

To See Ourselves as We Really Are

The second advantage of regular accountability is that it allows us to see ourselves as we really are before God. When we place ourselves in a vulnerable position that requires total transparency and absolute authenticity, we have no other option than to see ourselves as we truly are.

> *As iron sharpens iron,*
> *so one man sharpens another.*
> *As water reflects a face,*
> *so a man's heart reflects the man*
> (Proverbs 27:17, 19).

As we hear the words of our accountability partners, we must remember those words come from what is in a person's heart. We must also use Scripture to set the person back on the right course. As in any area of life, the key to this confrontation is balance. The Bible never says to speak the truth without love, to confront the brother, berate him and make him feel lower than life. In our quest to confront and call sin "sin," we may leave the brother feeling like a loser. Neither does the Bible say we should sugarcoat the truth about sin by saying, "Oh, it's OK. Don't worry about it. Everyone falls to that sort of thing." That leaves the brother feeling like God is a wimp and there is no need for repentance. The Bible says we need to speak the truth "in love." That is the necessary balance in accountability groups. We call sin "sin," but we do it by putting our arm around the brother or sister to give him or her a hand up from a fallen state.

We Won't Get Away with Our Sinful Habits

The third advantage of accountability is that we are not as likely to get away with the sinful habits and poor choices we make on a regular basis. Proverbs 27:5–6 says, *Better is open rebuke / than hidden love. / Wounds from a friend can be trusted, / but an enemy multiplies kisses.*

What would we give to have a friend who can be trusted? The church is full of people who say they love, but the reality of their practice leaves us standing in a daze looking around saying, "Where is all that love?" Every time we see a brother stumble, we have tragically watched ten other "Christians" running to rub his face in his sin. The church is the only group known for shooting its wounded. That shouldn't be!

If accountability will ever work in the church, the level of trust for one another must improve. That is even truer with the most difficult hidden secrets of our lives, and it will not happen unless we turn the question around and ask ourselves the same questions. "Can I be trusted?" "Would another brother trust me enough to share something very personal, knowing I will not tell anyone?" "Does he know I will take that confession and do all I can to restore him to a right relationship with God and with those people who have been offended or affected?"

Questions to Assess Where We Stand

Accountability is necessary to win the spiritual race we have been called to run. Accountability has no boundaries. Presidents, pastors, parents, and pupils equally need to be accountable. So what do we do? We ask ourselves these questions so we can properly assess and evaluate where we stand as to our readiness to be a part of an accountability group—an ABS group:

1. Can I name someone outside my family to whom I have made myself accountable? Have I given that person abso-

lute freedom to ask deep penetrating questions into the character of who I really am?

2. Am I aware of the dangers of not being accountable? Arrogance will keep many people from accountability. Will I refuse to recognize blind spots or unhealthy relationships, bad habits, or maybe even bad motives?

3. When was the last time I gave an account for the private areas of my life to someone outside my family? This includes the following areas:

- Finance: Sizeable purchases and patterns of giving.

- Work Ethics: The time I spend at work, my attitude and my impact on others.

- Scheduled Activities: Maybe I am too busy. Maybe I am lazy.

- Lust: Do I struggle with pornography in DVD rentals, magazines, novels, the Internet, or my entertainment lifestyle?

A Special Note to Christian Leaders

None of us is above temptation. The world in which we live is a battlefield. There are tough issues we must be ready to tackle head on. Those of us who hold positions of leadership in our churches must understand that we may be the ones whom the enemy will attack first. We need always to be on guard! We can fail like anyone else. We cannot be so proud as to overlook the battle of the flesh going on in our own souls. How can we constantly point out the speck of wood in someone else's eye when we have a plank in our own (cf. Matt. 7:4)?

Let us move beyond our comfort zones and establish systems and vehicles that will allow for authentic accountability. This will not harm the church; it will strengthen it. We cannot expect our people to place themselves into regular accountability groups when we don't model it ourselves. Values are caught, not taught. We must lead by example. There may be consequences to our sin, but God's Word is clear that God's desire is not to take the position of leadership away from us. Look at King David, who was considered a man after God's own heart. Here was a man who had committed adultery and murder. God did not oust him from his position. Why? Because God saw David's true heart. Psalm 51: 6–17 is clear:

> *Surely you desire truth in the inner parts;*
> *   you teach me wisdom in the inmost place.*
> *   Cleanse me with hyssop, and I will be clean;*
> *   wash me, and I will be whiter than snow…*
> *Create in me a pure heart, O God,*
> *   and renew a steadfast spirit within me.*
> *Do not cast me from your presence*
> *   or take your Holy Spirit from me.*
> *Restore to me the joy of your salvation*
> *   and grant me a willing spirit, to sustain me.*
> *Then I will teach transgressors your ways,*
> *   and sinners will turn back to you.*
> *Save me from bloodguilt, O God,*
> *   the God who saves me,*
> *   and my tongue will sing of your righteousness.*
> *O Lord, open my lips,*
> *   and my mouth will declare your praise.*
> *You do not delight in sacrifice, or I would bring it;*
> *   you do not take pleasure in burnt offerings.*
> *The sacrifices of God are a broken spirit;*
> *   a broken and contrite heart,*
> *   O God, you will not despise.*

This prayer of King David is awe-inspiring. I know it as well as any other part of the Bible. What was David saying? Look at his conclusion. Nothing David could *do* was good enough.

God desired that David's heart be broken, that David would have a contrite heart! "Contrite" is another word for repentant. What God wants from us is a turning away from the ways of the world and making an about-face in the direction of His glorious light.

There is a principle that we can apply to our lives as we learn a lesson from a message originally directed to the people of Israel. *"If my people, who are called by my name, will humble themselves and pray and seek my face and turn from their wicked ways, then will I hear from heaven and will forgive their sin and will heal their land"* (2 Chronicles 7:14).

Leaders, we need to follow the example of David. We are to humble ourselves and make ourselves accountable to God and to others. David must have entered into an accountability relationship with Nathan. Why else would Nathan have risked his life to approach and confront the king with the accusation that he had violated his character? There is an implied level of trust in that relationship. David was a wise leader. He allowed men in his life to speak even the hardest of truth so he could remain a man after God's own heart.

Lessons of Love Learned when a Brother Falls

"Everyone makes mistakes," we are told. But I don't have to make all of them. There are plenty of mistakes to be made by everyone. In the area of morality, it would be wise to learn some of the tougher lessons by looking at the mistakes of others. Remember, but for the grace of God any of us could fall.

Most of us have watched a brother fall, perhaps in the media or maybe a bit closer—someone whom we know personally. It helps to take a look inside a story of failure, to get a personal exposé on what was going on inside the hearts of men or women who have fallen.

On the surface everything about these persons looks grand. Here are men or women whom we all respect. They may even have taken others to great spiritual heights. They seem to have a growing influence in the Kingdom of God. Little did we know that brewing under their smiling façade was a secret that was, as one fallen leader stated, "so repulsive and dark that I've been warring against it all of my adult life."

The news of a respected leader's scandalous fall comes crashing into our lives like a truck hitting us head-on. The pain of seeing another brother in Christ fall so fast and so hard, combined with the tremendous loss of credibility that the church or organization faces, is enough to make any follower of Jesus sick.

What is so gripping for those of us who desire to pursue ABS of Faith is not just the sin that was committed but also the fallen leader's initial denials. With a fall of this magnitude come lies and cover-up attempts that are obvious to almost any observer. There is much to be learned from those who have fallen.

One fallen leader, when his sin had been found out, said it all too well:

The fact is, I am guilty of sexual immorality, and I take responsibility for the entire problem. I am a deceiver and a liar. For extended periods of time, I would enjoy victory and rejoice in freedom. Then, from time to time, the dirt that I thought was gone would resurface, and I would find myself thinking thoughts and experiencing desires that were contrary to everything I believe and teach. Through the years, I've sought assistance in a variety of ways, with none of them proving to be effective in me. Then, because of pride, I began deceiving those I love the most because I didn't want to hurt or disappoint them.

Many who are struggling with sin in their lives feel a need to live a lie because of all they feel is at stake in their lives—primarily family and ministry. In that moment of truth, when sin is revealed and comes to the light, the person's ministry and credibility are shattered. The fallen one may have never brought anyone into his or her circle of trust, someone who loved him or her enough to speak hard truth in love when it was needed.

I am convinced that the day the sin is revealed in any person's life, although it is in a very real sense a horrible day—one of the worst days of his life—it is equally the most freeing day of that person's life. The lie is over. Darkness is exposed and the marvelous light of God's glorious grace is brought into his life. He is now ready to receive the greatest gift from God—grace. God is full of it, grace upon grace. He cannot be emptied of it. He wants us to experience real life, a gift of His grace—free from guilt.

Learning from the Tragedies

What can we learn from these tragedies so we won't make the same mistakes? Here are a few critical lessons for all of us.

We are not above mistakes ourselves. The fall of any brother or sister in the faith is a paramount call to repentance and restoration for each of us. It is a call for accountability and authenticity. It is a call to you and to me. Why? Because we are not above falling into any sin ourselves. Maybe our category of sexual temptation is not homosexuality or heterosexual adultery. Perhaps our struggle is Internet pornography, lustful thoughts toward a co-worker or a congregant, or a relationship with a member of the opposite or same sex that has crossed that invisible line of appropriateness into a downward slide into irreparable compromise.

If David, "a man after God's own heart," could aggressively pursue Bathsheba and kill her husband in the aftermath of a quick cover-up, any of us could too. Our Bathsheba may not be bathing in full view of our second-story window, but her bubble bath is ready to run hot on that computer screen or movie screen of our depraved minds. No wonder the great apostle Paul wrote in Romans 7:14–25:

> *We know that the law is spiritual; but I am unspiritual, sold as a slave to sin. I do not understand what I do. For what I want to do I do not do, but what I hate I do. And if I do what I do not want to do, I agree that the law is good. As it is, it is no longer I myself who do it, but it is sin living in me. I know that nothing good lives in me, that is, in my sinful nature. For I have the desire to do what is good, but I cannot carry it out. For what I do is not the good I want to do; no, the evil I do not want to do—this I keep on doing. Now if I do what I do not want to do, it is no longer I who do it, but it is sin living in me that does it.*
>
> *So I find this law at work: When I want to do good, evil is right there with me. For in my inner being I delight in God's law; but I see another law at work in the members of my body, waging war against the law of my mind and making me a prisoner of the law of sin at work within my members. What a wretched man I am! Who will rescue me from this body of death? Thanks be to God—through Jesus Christ our Lord!*

I thank God for this passage because it reminds me that even the apostle Paul had nagging sins that he constantly battled against. If one of the greatest figures of the Old Testament, David, and another of the New Testament, Paul, battled against the temptation to sin, we can be sure that we are not above the battle. As a matter of fact, as soon as we think we are, that's when we are most vulnerable. Paul gives this warning to us: *So, if you think you are standing firm, be careful that you don't fall!* (1 Corinthians 10:12).

You and I are not above any sin. The same robe of depravity clothes us until the day we exchange it for a robe of righteousness when we get to heaven.

We need to choose to be completely accountable and authentic with somebody we trust. We've read the verse, *Therefore confess your sins to each other and pray for each other so that you may be healed* (James 5:16). Notice what the verse is not saying. It's not saying we should confess every sin to everyone. But it seems it is quite clearly saying there should be, at the very least, one trusted person in our lives who knows about our dirty laundry.

For me that man is Mike Silliman. He was an elder in the church I pastor. Today he pastors a church our church planted, the Elk Creek Community Church, 20 minutes from us. He is my ABS partner. He is a personal friend, colleague, and fellow struggler. Mike knows all my struggles. He keeps me accountable, prays for me, rebukes me from time to time, and encourages me all the time. I thank God for him. I praise the Lord there is someone in my life to whom I can be totally accountable on every level.

But not all of us have such a person in our lives, someone we can completely trust and with whom we can be 100 percent vulnerable. If we don't, we need to seek such a person right away. Ideally we need to find a godly, close friend and ask him to hold us accountable. Give that accountability partner specific questions to ask (whatever our area of weakness or potential struggle). Give that person permission to ask the tough questions anytime. This kind of no-holds-barred accountability is a must for every minister of the gospel.

We need to remove as many sin opportunities as possible. If someone struggles with Internet porn late at night in his study, he needs to choose to avoid computer use late at night. If any of us is attracted to a certain woman in our church who needs counseling, why not delegate that counseling opportunity to a women's ministry leader or associate pastor?

Romans 13:14 (NKJV) tells us, *But put on the Lord Jesus Christ, and make no provision for the flesh, to fulfill its lusts.*

I can't trust only in accountability and personal rules to keep myself pure. One well-known counselor said it this way,

"I have counseled countless pastors across America who have fallen into sexual sin. Every single one of those pastors who fell had some sort of accountability and personal rules to keep them from sexual compromise."[1]

Here are Paul's words in Colossians 2:20–23 (NLT):

You have died with Christ, and he has set you free from the evil powers of this world. So why do you keep on following rules of the world, such as, "Don't handle, don't eat, don't touch." Such rules are mere human teaching about things that are gone as soon as we use them. These rules may seem wise because they require strong devotion, humility, and severe bodily discipline. But they have no effect when it comes to conquering a person's evil thoughts and desires.

Character Cannot Be Manufactured

Some have come to believe that character can be manufactured. That is not true. If I desire the character of God to be evidenced in my life, the Word must dwell in my heart. Ephesians 3:17–19 encourages us: *So that Christ may dwell in your hearts through faith. And I pray that you, being rooted and established in love, may have power, together with all the saints, to grasp how wide and long and high and deep is the love of Christ, and to know this love that surpasses knowledge—that you may be filled to the measure of all the fullness of God.*

The Word that lives in my heart will produce and give me His character. I cannot work for His character. He produces it as I abide in Him. I am truly the only person who can hold myself accountable. The level of accountability and the quality of my character depend solely on my intimacy with the Written and Living Word—Jesus!

[1] H. B. London, "Shepherd's Covenant E-letter."

Part Two

Chapter 5

Bible Reading

"It's a lovely book!" Some have one copy of it and others have 21. In the home where I grew up we had a big one and it sat on the living room table. I remember as a kid getting one with a picture of Jesus on it, and on His lap sat lots of little children. I grew older and my parents gave me my first leather-bound book. It had pages like no other book I had; they were almost like silk.

As I went to church I noticed many people carrying this book under their arms. In my former church they even had a lot of these books sitting in little shelves on the back of each pew. In my new church, we seldom use the book because now they put the words of the book on a big screen. What is the significance of this book?

When I was a youth pastor, parents came to ask me what version of this book they should purchase for their children. My response was always the same: "Whichever one they will read." That is the purpose of the book; it is to be read. The book is not to be worshiped. The Author of its words is to be worshiped.

The content is not intended to be informative; its message is to be fleshed out. This book should revolutionize and transform our lives. It is not how much of the book we know that counts, but how obedient we are to its message and commands.

I have met people over the years who refuse to acknowledge the truth of this book. They say, "I don't believe in the Bible!" I ask, "Have you ever read it?" They respond, "No!" That is a statement of ignorance. How can people believe or not believe in something they have not read? I challenge people to dig into its pages. It is the story of Jesus Christ. Our lives will be changed because we will come face to face with our Creator. We will be left with a choice—to accept Him or reject Him. The wonder of that statement is that the Creator gives us the opportunity to make that choice for ourselves.

A few times each year, in our church, we do what we call "Harp and Bowl" worship experiences, or open worship experiences. (See Revelation 5:8 where "harp" speaks of God's music and worship songs and the "bowl" speaks of intercession or prayers of the saints.) Many things can happen during these times, but one of the most profound is that people from all walks of life stand to testify to how relevant God's Word is to their lives. They will share a Scripture and the entire congregation is encouraged—or challenged. Both encouragement and challenge are realities. Some would like to read only those portions of Scripture that fit their lifestyle, but we must adhere to the whole counsel of God's Word. This book touches on every part of our lives.

Many of us would like to be well prepared at every point and fully equipped to do good to everyone. How can we learn to do that? The answer is in 2 Timothy 3:16–17, *The whole Bible was given to us by inspiration from God and is useful to teach us what is true and to make us realize what is wrong in our lives; it straightens us out and helps us do what is right. It is God's way of making us well prepared at every point, fully equipped to do good to everyone* (TLB).

That's the purpose of the Bible. It teaches us what is true. It makes us realize what is wrong in our lives. It straightens us out when we wander off the path. And it's God's way of preparing us at every point, fully equipped to do good to everyone.

We must learn how to feed ourselves on the Word of God. There's an old saying that "If you give a man a fish, you've fed him for a day, but if you teach a man to fish, you've fed him for a lifetime." We need to learn how to fish, to catch for ourselves the truths in Scripture that can nurture us. Here are the fundamentals, the basics of how to get into God's Word.

Six Ways to Handle Your Bible

I remember, as a little boy in Sunday school, how I learned to label my five fingers.

On my little finger I wrote the word "Hear."
On my next finger I wrote the word "Read."
On my third finger I wrote the word "Study."
On my index finger I wrote the word "Memorize"
On my thumb I wrote the word "Meditate."

To complete the hand, I wrote the word "Apply" down the middle of my palm.

These are the six ways that we can handle God's Word: Hear, Read, Study, Memorize, Meditate, and Apply.

When I handle God's Word, I want to have more than just the little finger; I want the whole hand. Some Christians take the Bible into their lives only by what they hear; they don't read the Bible or study it. They go to church, but they just hear the Bible read. If I try to hold my Bible with just my little finger, it's not much of a grasp. How easy it is for the Word of God to be pulled away from my grasp. If I decide not only to hear the Word of God but also to read the Bible every day, I now have two fingers with which to grasp the Bible. The devil can still pull it out of my grip, but it's a little bit harder. If I am studying the Bible, I am now getting a little better grip on the Bible. It can still be taken away, but not as easily.

Memorizing is harder. How much do we tend to forget when we memorize? Very little. Then when we add the "meditate" finger and the whole "apply" hand, we have it all. We now have a firm grasp. But if all we are doing is hearing the Word of God, we're not getting very much. The more the "five fingers and the hand" are wrapped around the Bible, the better grasp we're going to have of God's Word.

How to Hear God's Word

Romans 10:17 says, *So faith comes from hearing, and hearing by the word of Christ* (NASB). Many of us want to have more faith. The way to have more faith is to hear the Word of God. That is the easiest way to get into God's Word. It's the most common way. But it's also the way in which we can lose the most content.

Here are some ways to hear God's Word: Listen to the Bible on CD, at church services, in Bible studies, by recorded sermons, or through radio/television teachers. Every day we can turn on the radio and hear great Bible teachers such as Chuck Swindoll, Chuck Smith, Charles Stanley, or John MacArthur. With modern technology we can podcast or download great messages into our MP3 players. Some of today's most innovative communicators are a click away. We can hear Andy Stanley or Louie Giglio, Erwin McManus, Craig Groeschel, Francis Chan, or Rob Bell. Hearing God's Word today is easier than it has ever been for most of us in this country.

Those are all good ways to hear God's Word. But the problem is that within 72 hours, we tend to forget 95 percent of what we hear. That's why we can go to church week after week, year after year, and not really grow. We don't really remember what we heard. How can we apply it if we don't remember it?

Improving Our Hearing

We need to be ready and eager to hear God. Jesus said, *He who has ears to hear, let him hear,* (Matt. 11:15 NASB). *Be quick to listen* (James 1:19). When we go to church or to a Bible study, we ought to prepare our hearts to hear. We should go, praying, "Lord, I want to be ready to hear."

We must deal with attitudes that prevent hearing God. Remember the parable of the sower in which Jesus says, *Therefore consider carefully how you listen* (Luke 8:18). In that parable, Jesus talks about having a closed mind (any fear, pride or bitterness that prevents hearing God) or a superficial mind. That's the mind where the seed falls onto the shallow soil and springs up quickly, but there is hard bedrock underneath (am I really serious about hearing God speak?). Or we can have a preoccupied mind (am I too busy and concerned with other things in life to concentrate on what God has to say?). I need to deal with those kinds of attitudes in order to hear.

I need to confess any sin in my life. James 1:21 tells us, *Therefore, get rid of all moral filth and the evil that is so prevalent and humbly accept the word planted in you, which can save you.*

When a woman has her nails done, she knows that before an attendant puts on the new nail polish she has to remove the old. James is telling us to first get rid of all the garbage in our lives so God can fill our lives with His Word. We have to put off the old before we can put on the new... *and humbly accept the word* (James 1:21). When I'm not getting anything out of a message, I need to ask, "What's wrong with me? Am I not tuned in to God?"

I need to take notes on what I hear. *We must pay more careful attention, therefore, to what we have heard, so that we do not drift away* (Hebrews 2:1).

It helps to keep a spiritual notebook, a tool to help organize and retain the blessings of God. It's one of the basic disciplines that will help us to hear the Word of God. We write it down. Remember that most of us have a good forgetter!

We act on what we hear. *Do not merely listen to the word, and so deceive yourselves. Do what it says* (James 1:22). In verse

25 we read, *But the man who looks intently into the perfect law that gives freedom, and continues to do this, not forgetting what he has heard, but doing it—he will be blessed in what he does.*

The Bible is saying that if I want really to be blessed when I hear a Bible study or sermon, I need to put it into practice.

Some people define their discipleship as attending formal Bible study groups. That is informational at best. We have a lot of "fat" Christians who know lots of biblical content. The true definition of discipleship is to be "doers of the Word." The Bible says, *From everyone who has been given much, much will be demanded; and from the one who has been entrusted with much, much more will be asked* (Luke 12:48).

Adding to Our Grip

First we had only the little pinky finger; now we have to involve the ring finger too. We don't simply listen to the reading of God's Word; we read it for ourselves. How are we to read God's Word? The Bible says in Revelation 1:3, *Blessed is the one who reads the words of this prophecy, and blessed are those who hear it and take to heart what is written in it, because the time is near.*

How often should I read God's Word? Daily. *[The Scriptures] shall be his constant companion. He must read from it every day of his life so that he will learn to respect the Lord his God by obeying all of his commands* (Deut. 17:19 TLB). God wants me to read the Word on a daily basis.

Here are some suggestions on how to read the Word of God. First, read it systematically. Don't use the dip and skip method. Many of us have done that. We sit down on the edge of our bed at night and start to feel guilty—"I've got to read my Bible!" So we start wherever it opens.

The story is told of a man who said, "Lord, I want to know your will for my life." He opened up his Bible and put his finger down and it said, "Judas went out and hanged himself." He thought, "That can't be right." So he closed his Bible and opened it again and put his finger down and it said, "Go thou and do likewise." He thought, "Lord, this cannot be right. Two out of three…" He opened it a third time and put his finger down and it said, "And what thou doest, do quickly."

We need to choose a book of the Bible and read it, the whole book, before turning to another book. When I read a letter I don't read the last part, then the first part, then the middle. I read it straight through. Many of the books in the New Testament are letters. They are meant to be read straight through.

We should read the whole Bible systematically, not just our favorite parts. Some of us get stuck in Psalms and Proverbs and the Gospels. It's going to be pretty embarrassing when we get to heaven and Habakkuk comes up and says, "How did you like my book?" and we didn't even know it was in the Bible. Read the whole Bible—Matthew, Mark, Luke, John, and all the other inspired writers.

I have many Bibles in which I've taken notes; many of the verses have notations by them. But when I want to have a serious quiet time with God, I use a Bible without notes, because when I use a Bible with my notes or a study Bible, I tend to see the same things over and over. When I'm reading through passages in my quiet time, I need a Bible that has no notes at all so I can see something fresh, and when I do, I record my discoveries in a journal.

There are some great modern translations for reading. The *Good News* translation is excellent and very readable. The American Bible Society translated the *Good News Bible*. Its original purpose was to teach English as a second language overseas. A newer translation is *The New Living Translation*. It is a scholarly translation of Scripture that reads much like its popular paraphrase counterpart, *The Living Bible*. Both have very simple vocabularies.

I find it helpful to read the Bible quietly by myself. When my mind starts to wander while I'm reading, I just read out loud. My mind is less prone to wander when I'm reading the Bible aloud. It also helps to choose a reading plan and stick with it.

At the end of this chapter there are several reading plans. One will enable you to read through the entire New Testament in about 30 days. I know people who think nothing of reading their Sunday newspaper from cover to cover, and most major newspapers have more words in the Sunday edition than are in the New Testament. But when I suggest, "Why don't you read through the New Testament?" they reply, "Oh, no. That's too long."

There are other reading plans as well. Each of us can keep a record for ourselves as we read through the Bible in a year. If I pace myself and read approximately 15 minutes a day, I can read through the Bible once a year. I have encouraged people who have never done it to make it their goal. Do I believe the entire Bible? Have I read it from cover to cover? How can I know that I believe the Bible from cover to cover if I have never read it cover to cover?

Several publishers have made reading the Bible in a year a much simpler task. They have compiled some Old Testament and New Testament readings and added some Psalms and a Proverb to a daily reading plan. If you read the assigned portion each day, in a year's time you can read the entire Bible. My ABS partner and I are currently doing that together. It is wonderful.

Adding the Next Finger to My Grip

Writing about the Berean church, Luke tells us, *Now the Bereans were of more noble character than the Thessalonians, for they received the message with great eagerness and examined the Scriptures every day to see if what Paul said was true* (Acts 17:11).

The Bereans were commended because they didn't just accept what was told them as the truth. They looked at the

Scriptures every day to make sure that the preaching and teaching agreed with the Bible. We are to do the same. We don't just accept what a Bible teacher tells us, because to really know God's Word we study to see whether what is being taught is verified there. *Do your best to present yourself to God as one approved, a workman who does not need to be ashamed and who correctly handles the word of truth (*2 Timothy 2:15). We are to know what His Word says and means. How do we do that? We know only by studying it.

Anyone can learn how to study the Bible. It is not a skill reserved for professional theologians. God intended each of us to study His Word, not just hear it and read it.

The difference between reading and studying the Bible is that studying involves using a pencil. You need to keep a pencil and a piece of paper ready to take notes on what you discover. The secret of effective Bible study is in knowing how to ask the right questions. You might look at a passage of Scripture and not know where to begin, but here are some questions to ask—basic journalistic questions that can apply to any passage of Scripture and gain insight from it. Who? What? When? Where? Why? How?

You can look at a passage of Scripture and ask yourself, "Who is a disciple in this passage of Scripture? This says so-and-so did this. So this is what a disciple is. What are the results of being a disciple? Why should I even attempt to be a disciple? How do I become a disciple?" When you look at a passage of Scripture, ask those questions and write down what you discover. It is a very simple way to begin studying, but it will help you start.

This is just touching the tip of the iceberg about studying the Bible. One of the simplest yet thorough books on learning how to study the Bible is Rick Warren's, *Dynamic Bible Study Methods.* It's an excellent resource designed for the average person.

Everybody needs at least one study Bible. Here are four of the best:

1. For personal application, *The Life Application Bible*, published by Tyndale, is great. It has all kinds of application questions for us after we read a passage. It helps us to think through what we've just read.

2. A good topical Study Bible is the *Thompson Chain Reference Bible*. The value of this type of Bible is that it is organized by topics. You simply look up a word, and it will point you to all the references in the Bible that use that word.

3. The *NIV Study Bible* is a good background study Bible. This Bible often gives you the author, the date of writing, and more detail about the background and purpose of each book. It explores themes and theologically significant points. It also includes outlines.

4. *The Ryrie Study Bible* is a fantastic study tool. In using a study Bible, remember the notes are not inspired. They represent the author's positions: in this case, Charles Ryrie's. The notes provide help, especially to the student with little experience in Bible study. This volume includes excellent outlines, book introductions, and quality notes on difficult passages. The book concludes with a lengthy "Synopsis of Bible Doctrine."

With any study aid remember that the Holy Spirit should always be your first teacher.

Using a variety of Bible translations can be helpful, also. One good tool is *Any Translation New Testament*. Its format includes eight translations side-by-side, including the King James Version (KJV), The Living Bible (TLV), Good News, the New American Standard Bible (NASB), the New International Version (NIV), and Phillips translation. This excellent tool helps save the student from having to spread out eight different Bibles on his desk to make comparisons.

A complete concordance, corresponding with the translation of the Bible being used, is a tool every serious Christian needs. A concordance lists every use of every word in the Bible. For example, if the verse you're looking for has "love" in it, you can look up "love" in the alphabetical listing and find all the places that word is used.

A Bible dictionary and a Bible encyclopedia offer a lot of detail. They are fun to read. I find facts in them I've never heard before. If I have a question about a subject, I go to the Bible dictionary to find the information I need. A search of online resources will provide many of these tools for immediate use.

Bible commentaries are useful tools, too. A Bible commentary offers the observations of the author (often a professional theologian), explaining what a verse of Scripture means. Commentaries may include studies of the whole Bible or they may focus on particular books or segments of the Bible. They can be a great help. But if you go there first, you rob yourself of the joy of making discoveries on your own.

One other help might be a Bible atlas, such as the *Moody Atlas of Bible Lands*. It has maps, charts, and documentation that help us to understand something about Israel, Palestine, Egypt, and other biblical places.

Many of these tools are available online, and a search will yield a great many helpful resources.

Adding the Index Finger to My Grip of the Bible

The Bible on the shelf does me no good at all. It has all the answers for my life, but if I don't have it in my life it doesn't make much difference. So the more Scripture I absorb into my mind the stronger my ABS of Faith will be.

Follow my advice, my son; always keep it in mind and stick to it. Obey me and live! Guard my words as your most precious possession. Write them down, and also keep them deep within your heart (Proverbs 7:1–3 TLB). Nothing will do more for your spiritual life than memorizing Scripture. One of the most powerful habits any Christian can develop is to memorize God's Word.

As we fill our minds with Scripture, we soon discover His Word comes to mind when we need it most.

A key benefit of memorizing Scripture is that it helps me to resist temptation. Jesus' experience in the wilderness is the great example. When the devil tempted Him, Jesus quoted Scripture He had memorized.

When temptation comes—and it will come—we need to turn our "I know I shouldn't" into the declaration, "It is written!"

The psalmist declared, *I have hidden your word in my heart / that I might not sin against you* (Psalm 119:11). And again in Psalm 119:133, *Establish my footsteps in Your word, / And do not let any iniquity have dominion over me* (NASB).

Memorizing Scripture helps to make wise decisions. It is true that *[God's] word is a lamp to my feet / and a light for my path* (Psalm 119:105).

Most of us can remember times we have thought or prayed, "Lord, what am I going to do now?" Then a helpful verse of Scripture popped into our minds. That's because we had it memorized.

Memorized Scripture is there in my mind to strengthen me when I'm under stress. *But now, Lord, what do I look for? / My hope is in you* (Psalm 39:7). When we're tense, nervous, or uptight, God brings to mind a verse we have memorized. When we become so busy, and our busyness saps our strength, we are able to say, "Lord, I need strength to make it through the rest of this day." In answer to that prayer, He may remind us of a verse such as Isaiah 40:31, *But those who hope in the LORD / will renew their strength. / They will soar on wings like eagles; / they will run and not grow weary, / they will walk and not be faint.*

Memorized Scripture is there to comfort me when I'm sad. *Your words are what sustain me. They are food to my hungry soul. They bring joy to my sorrowing heart and delight me* (Jer. 15:16 TLB). Notice Proverbs 22:18: *For it is pleasing when you keep them in your heart and have all of them ready on your lips.*

When I am speaking to someone about his or her need of the Savior, memorized Scripture helps with my witness. Peter urges, *Always be prepared to give an answer to everyone who asks you to give the reason for the hope that you have* (1 Peter 3:15). When somebody comes to me and asks, "What does the Bible say about...." or "How do you know that?" and I have verses memorized about those issues, it will make me more effective.

Specific truths should be memorized to combat specific temptations and lies. Here are some examples:

1. Believing that sin has no consequences for me – James 1:15
2. Dishonesty – Colossians 3:9
3. An unforgiving spirit – Matthew 6:14
4. Pride – Jeremiah 9:23
5. Fear of change – Romans 12:2
6. Anger and revenge – James 1:20
7. Unwholesome language – Ephesians 4:29
8. Selfishness – Philippians 2:3
9. Materialism – Proverbs 30:8
10. Authority – Romans 13:1
11. Choice of friends – Proverbs 13:20

There are certain helps when memorizing Scripture.

Pick a verse that speaks to you.
That's probably the verse God wants you to memorize next. Start with that verse. Then move on to others.

Say the verse reference before and after.
The hardest part to remember is the reference, the address. "Where in the world is that verse?" So we say it at the start and at the end.

Read the verse aloud many times.
Record it. We memorize a verse by saying it aloud. We don't memorize by only reading it; our ears have a lot to do with what we memorize.

Break the verse into natural phrases.

Memorize word for word. Don't break up the thought. Usually there is a clause or a natural pause. Repeat that phrase over and over and then move on to the next thought or clause. Then you can combine them until the entire verse is memorized.

Emphasize key words when quoting the verse.

One way that's kind of fun (I've done this with kids) is to write down a verse and then erase one word at a time. By the time you have every word erased, you've memorized it.

Write the verse on flash cards.

Carry those cards at all times. When you have a few minutes, you can pull them out for review.

Display those verses in prominent places where you will see them.

Paste them on the bathroom mirror, over your desk, by your computer, or wherever you are likely to see them often.

Always memorize the verse word perfect.

Memorize it exactly the way it is written.

Put the verse to music.

Some people can write a song using a verse. That's effective.

Get a partner to help.

When you have someone to help you, check your recollection, challenge you, and learn with you so you can also challenge and check up on that person, good memorization happens.

Some people argue, "I just can't memorize anything" But that's not true. Some of those same people have no difficulty remembering other things that are important to them. Some men can quote athletic statistics for the past 20 years; there are teenagers who can quote the top ten songs for the last five years. We memorize the phone numbers of our friends. We remember what we're interested in. If we're interested in memorizing Scripture, we will be able to remember it.

How important was Bible memorization to David? David wrote, *The law from your mouth is more precious to me than thousands of pieces of silver and gold* (Psalm 119:72). That's how important God's Word ought to be to us too.

These essential memorization exercises will give each one of us the ABS of Faith we are looking for. We will be rooted and founded in the Word of God.

Gripping the Bible with the Thumb

The thumb wraps around the Bible. It is like our meditation, which is focused thinking about a Bible verse in order to discover how we can apply its truth to our lives. The word for meditation is also the word for rumination. Rumination is the process in which a cow chews its cud, swallows it, regurgitates it, chews it again, and swallows it, going through that process about seven times. A cow does that to get every bit of nourishment possible from the grass.

That's what we're to do with God's Word. We are to focus our thinking, spend time on it trying to drain every bit of spiritual nourishment and food we can from the Word of God.

We are already people who meditate. Most of us are great worriers. A worrier meditates. Worrying is just negative meditation. When we are worrying about something, what are we doing? We're ruminating on it. We're thinking about it. We lie in bed and think and think—and go through what is on our minds in every way that we can. That's negative meditation.

Meditation is the key to becoming more like Christ. Proverbs 4:23 instructs us, *Above all else, guard your heart, for it affects everything you do* (NLT).

We become what we think about. If we want to become like Christ, we must spend time thinking about Him. Paul tells us to be *transformed by the renewing of your mind* (Romans 12:2). When we meditate on Scripture, and on the Lord, God is able to renew our minds and replace bad thoughts with good. As we think deeply about the Lord and His Word, we become more and more like Him.

Meditation is often the key to answered prayer. Jesus said, *But if you stay joined to me and my words remain in you, you may ask any request you like, and it will be granted!* (John 15:7 (NLT). What is the condition? If we are living in His Word and His words are living in us, then we can ask what we want and it will happen. The more we know Christ, the more our thoughts become His thoughts. So we can have confidence when we pray because we know that what we are praying is according to God's will. We're confident our own mind is in alignment with His and we're not going to be asking for something totally out of His will.

Meditation is a key to successful living. God challenged Joshua, *"Do not let this Book of the Law depart from your mouth; meditate on it day and night, so that you may be careful to do everything written in it. Then you will be prosperous and successful"* (Joshua 1:8).

We are to meditate on the Word day and night so we may be careful to do everything written in it. Then we will be prosperous and successful. This is the only promise of success in the Bible where the word "success" actually appears. If we meditate on God's Word, we will have success. It's tied into meditation. Again, "what you think about is what you become." If you are thinking about the Lord Jesus and His ways and becoming like Him, you will have success and live in a successful way. You will love people instead of reacting negatively to them. You will be honest in business.

These are simple ways to meditate on Scripture. We can picture it, visualizing the scene in our mind. This works really well on the narrative passages of Scripture, those that tell a story. An example is the episode of the woman at the well. What was it like for a woman who had been married five times, who was now living with a man who was not her husband, to have a stranger sit down and tell her about her life as though He'd known her forever? What feelings did that stir up in her? We can picture the scene in our minds and write down our thoughts.

We can say the verse out loud, each time emphasizing a different word. For example, Philippians 4:13 (NLT) states, *For I can do everything with the help of Christ who gives me the strength I need.* So we say, *I* can do all things through Christ—*me*! Not just Billy Graham or somebody I think is really terrific, but God says that *I* can do all things. Then *can do*. "I *can do* all things through Christ who strengthens me." It gives me hope and encouragement that God says I can do it. "I can do *all* things through Christ who strengthens me." Not just the easy things, but also the tough things. When we emphasize different words as we read through a verse, we discover a new meaning each time we do it.

I can rewrite the verse in my own words. If I am having a hard time understanding what a verse means and I can put that verse into my own words, it will give me a better idea of its meaning. Some people are good at taking the Word of God and putting it into their own words. It's a great discipline and it helps them meditate. Jesus knew Scripture and its principles well enough that He could always pull a story from His mind. If we can articulate a verse by paraphrasing it, we likely understand what the text is saying.

The Bible is personal; it is God's Word to us. So we can replace the pronouns or people in the verse with our own name. We can put our name in a promise. This is particularly helpful if we are feeling discouraged and starting to think God's Word was maybe meant for everyone else but not for us. When we put our name in a verse, it helps to reassure us that "God's Word is for me. He really did intend this word for me. This is a promise for me."

I can turn a verse into a prayer and pray it back to God. When I am reading in the Psalms, I can pray the words of

David, *O LORD, how long will you forget me? Forever? How long will you look the other way?* (Psalm 13:1 NLT). Perhaps on that day I feel the same way as the psalmist. I can take that prayer and pray it back to God.

Applying Scripture to Our Lives

In the center of my palm is the word "Apply." We must apply God's Word. Notice James 1:22: *Do not merely listen to the word, and so deceive yourselves. Do what it says.*

We also read, *Whoever practices and teaches these commands will be called great in the kingdom of heaven* (Matthew 5:19). This is the hardest part for many people. They wonder, "How do I apply Scripture?"

To apply Scripture, we can use what is called the application bridge. The application bridge helps us understand, "What did it mean then?" and move to "What does it mean now?" The bridge connecting these two questions is the key to understanding. It brings to light the timeless principle behind every story in the Bible. (No story is in the Bible by accident; even the most seemingly insignificant stories are there to teach a principle.) We can look behind the story, find the general principle, and apply that principle to today and beyond.

Here are the three questions to ask ourselves:

1. What did it mean to the original audience?
2. What is the underlying, timeless principle?
3. Where or how could I practice that principle today?

After we've discovered the principle, it helps to write a sentence to describe a project or action we will take to apply that truth. Most applications will focus on one of three relationships. When we're trying to apply the Bible to our life, we need to think relationships: Our relationship with God, our relationship with ourselves, and our relationship with other people.

There are four marks of a good application project:

1. It's personal
2. It's practical
3. It's possible
4. It's provable.

First, it's *personal*; that means *I* need to do it. When I think of an application in my quiet time, or when I'm studying the Bible and I'm ready to write what I am going to do about it, I put in the words, "I need to." I don't say, "they" or "you." It's "I."

Second, it's *practical*. If there is no practical reason to apply the Scripture, I will lack passion and drive to do so.

Third, if it's not *possible*, I'm just going to become discouraged. If I read 1 Thessalonians 5:17, *Pray without ceasing,* and I say, "I'm going to pray for every missionary in the world, every day," I am going to become discouraged. But I could say, "I will pray for *one* missionary every day." That's doable.

Finally, it's provable—I can prove that I've done it. That means I am to set a deadline. Then I've become a doer of the Word. The Bible says we are to be doers of the Word, not hearers only. Many times we go to Bible studies, read and hear the Scriptures, but we don't go home saying, "What am I to do about it?" We are to apply it.

Jesus said, Y*ou know these things—now do them! That is the path of blessing* (John 13:17 TLB). If we want to be blessed, we need to do these things.

What Do I Do in My Quiet Time?

Quiet time is a daily time set aside to be alone with God, to get to know Him through the Bible and prayer. Our time alone with God should be the top priority in our schedule. We cannot be healthy, growing Christians unless we spend time with God.

It's not just a good idea; it's a necessity. *Man does not live on bread alone, but on every word that comes from the mouth of God* (Matthew 4:4). What happens if we go a long time without food? We get sick. Eventually we will die. Food is a necessity. But physical food is not enough for us to be healthy. We must have spiritual intake of the Word of God.

Job got it! He declares, *"I have not departed from the command of His lips; I have treasured the words of His mouth more than my necessary food* (Job 23:12 NASB). He understood. Regular intake of the Word of God will keep us healthy and strong.

The Bible has a cleansing quality. Psalm 119:9, *How can a young man keep his way pure? / By living according to your word.* So our quiet time with God is like a spiritual bath. It's a time when we can be cleansed from the sin in our lives.

If I don't have a quiet time, I miss out on the purpose for which I was created. I'm rejecting the relationship that Jesus died to make possible in my life. I will never be like Jesus and experience His power, and I will never be used greatly by God. Instead I will remain a weak and sickly Christian. That alone should motivate us to have a quiet time.

Having a quiet time with God offers me an opportunity to do what Scripture says to do. *Watch the path of your feet, and all your ways will be established* (Proverbs 4:26 NASB).

I am to consider my way. I am to take time to be quiet and to assess my life. *In all your ways acknowledge Him, and He will make your paths straight* (Proverbs 3:6 NASB).

It means that I commit my day to Him. *Commit everything you do to the LORD. Trust him, and he will help you* (Psalm 37:5 NLT). After we've told the Lord we love Him and we've spent a little time looking over the goals we have for that day, we commit our schedule to Him: "Lord, I have this plan. This is what I think I'm supposed to be doing today. But only You really know where I'm supposed to be at 9:00 this morning or 2:30 this afternoon. These are the people I have on my list that I'm supposed to be with and talk to today. But you know the people You intend for me to be with." When we commit our schedule to the Lord like that, it helps us be more flexible and not get all bent out of shape when things don't go the way we think they should.

The objective of our quiet time is not to study about Christ so much as simply to spend time with Him. That's why we have two separate times: Bible study time and quiet time. Quiet time is to spend time with God. Bible study time is to learn about Him. The following pages provide several helps to assist you in your Bible reading.

My Time in the Word

The Christian life is similar to swimming upstream with your two strokes being Bible study and prayer. Take away one or both and you will lose momentum. There is no neutral area in this life. If you are not going forward, you must be going backward. Spending time in the Word of God is crucial for growth as a Christian. Look up the passages below and examine how to study your Bible.

Step One: Remove all sin

(James 1:21a) "Therefore, get rid of all moral filth and the evil that is so prevalent..."

Step Two: Remain open and teachable

(James l:21b) "...and humbly accept the word planted in you, which can save you."

Step Three: Read until you find something to do and then do it

(James 1:22) "Do not merely listen to the word, and so deceive yourselves. Do what is says."

Now it's your turn.

Use the following forms and begin today to spend time in the Word every day. Start in the book of John and study a chapter each day. That will last for three complete weeks. Follow these instructions:

1. Pray, confessing sin to God and asking Him to open your eyes to the truths in His Word.

2. Read through the entire chapter without interruption before answering any questions.

3. Write down what you feel is the main theme of the chapter. A main theme is simply the one thing the whole chapter is talking about.

4. Examine the chapter and write down any commands, examples and/or principles of truth about God that you find.

5. Write down at least three ways you can apply this passage to your life today.

_____

_____

_____

_____

My Time in the Word

Today's date: _____

Passage studied: _____

Observation

1. What is the main theme of this passage?

    _____

    _____

2. Are there any specific commands in this passage (something I should or should not do)?

    _____

    _____

3. Are there any positive examples that I should follow or any negative examples that I should avoid in this passage?

    _____

    _____

4. Are there any principles about the Christian life revealed in the passage?

_____

_____

5. Are there any truths mentioned about God's character in the passage?

_____

_____

Application

Based on my observation of this passage, what are three specific ways that I can apply this passage to my life today?

_____

_____

_____

☐ I have asked the Lord to help me to apply these areas to my life! (Check after prayer)

Through the New Testament in 30 Days

1. Matthew 1–9
2. Matthew 10–15
3. Matthew 16–22
4. Matthew 23–28
5. Mark 1–8
6. Mark 9–16
7. Luke 1–6
8. Luke 7–11
9. Luke 12–18
10. Luke 19–24
11. John 1–7
12. John 8–13
13. John 14–22
14. Acts 1–7
15. Acts 8–14
16. Acts 15–21
17. Acts 22–28
18. Romans 1–8
19. Romans 9–16
20. 1 Corinthians 1–9
21. 1 Corinthians 10–16
22. 2 Corinthians 1–13
23. Galatians–Ephesians
24. Philippians–2 Thessalonians
25. 1 Timothy–Philemon
26. Hebrews
27. James–2 Peter
28. 1 John–3 John
29. Revelation 1–11
30. Revelation 12–22

Old Testament and New Testament Check Off Sheet

Old Testament

Book	1	2	3	4	5	6	7	8	9	10	11	12	13	14	15	16	17	18	19	20
Genesis	1	2	3	4	5	6	7	8	9	10	11	12	13	14	15	16	17	18	19	20
	21	22	23	24	25	26	27	28	29	30	31	32	33	34	35	36	37	38	39	40
	41	42	43	44	45	46	47	48	49	50										
Exodus	1	2	3	4	5	6	7	8	9	10	11	12	13	14	15	16	17	18	19	20
	21	22	23	24	25	26	27	28	29	30	31	32	33	34	35	36	37	38	39	40
Leviticus	1	2	3	4	5	6	7	8	9	10	11	12	13	14	15	16	17	18	19	20
	21	22	23	24	25	26	27													
Numbers	1	2	3	4	5	6	7	8	9	10	11	12	13	14	15	16	17	18	19	20
	21	22	23	24	25	26	27	28	29	30	31	32	33	34	35	36				
Deuteronomy	1	2	3	4	5	6	7	8	9	10	11	12	13	14	15	16	17	18	19	20
	21	22	23	24	25	26	27	28	29	30	31	32	33	34						
Joshua	1	2	3	4	5	6	7	8	9	10	11	12	13	14	15	16	17	18	19	20
	21	22	23	24																
Judges	1	2	3	4	5	6	7	8	9	10	11	12	13	14	15	16	17	18	19	20
	21																			
Ruth	1	2	3	4																
1 Samuel	1	2	3	4	5	6	7	8	9	10	11	12	13	14	15	16	17	18	19	20
	21	22	23	24	25	26	27	28	29	30	31									
2 Samuel	1	2	3	4	5	6	7	8	9	10	11	12	13	14	15	16	17	18	19	20
	21	22	23	24																
1 Kings	1	2	3	4	5	6	7	8	9	10	11	12	13	14	15	16	17	18	19	20
	21	22																		
2 Kings	1	2	3	4	5	6	7	8	9	10	11	12	13	14	15	16	17	18	19	20
	21	22	23	24	25															
1 Chronicles	1	2	3	4	5	6	7	8	9	10	11	12	13	14	15	16	17	18	19	20
	21	22	23	24	25	26	27	28	29											
2 Chronicles	1	2	3	4	5	6	7	8	9	10	11	12	13	14	15	16	17	18	19	20
	21	22	23	24	25	26	27	28	29	30	31	32	33	34	35	36				
Ezra	1	2	3	4	5	6	7	8	9	10										
Nehemiah	1	2	3	4	5	6	7	8	9	10	11	12	13							
Esther	1	2	3	4	5	6	7	8	9	10										
Job	1	2	3	4	5	6	7	8	9	10	11	12	13	14	15	16	17	18	19	20
	21	22	23	24	25	26	27	28	29	30	31	32	33	34	35	36	37	38	39	40
	41	42																		

Old Testament

	1	2	3	4	5	6	7	8	9	10	11	12	13	14	15	16	17	18	19	20
Psalms	1	2	3	4	5	6	7	8	9	10	11	12	13	14	15	16	17	18	19	20
	21	22	23	24	25	26	27	28	29	30	31	32	33	34	35	36	37	38	39	40
	41	42	43	44	45	46	47	48	49	50	51	52	53	54	55	56	57	58	59	60
	61	62	63	64	65	66	67	68	69	70	71	72	73	74	75	76	77	78	79	80
	81	82	83	84	85	86	87	88	89	90	91	92	93	94	95	96	97	98	99	100
	101	102	103	104	105	106	107	108	109	110	111	112	113	114	115	116	117	118	119	120
	121	122	123	124	125	126	127	128	129	130	131	132	133	134	135	136	137	138	139	140
	141	142	143	144	145	146	147	148	149	150										
Proverbs	1	2	3	4	5	6	7	8	9	10	11	12	13	14	15	16	17	18	19	20
	21	22	23	24	25	26	27	28	29	30	31									
Ecclesiastes	1	2	3	4	5	6	7	8	9	10	11	12								
Sg of Solomon	1	2	3	4	5	6	7	8												
Isaiah	1	2	3	4	5	6	7	8	9	10	11	12	13	14	15	16	17	18	19	20
	21	22	23	24	25	26	27	28	29	30	31	32	33	34	35	36	37	38	39	40
	41	42	43	44	45	46	47	48	49	50	51	52	53	54	55	56	57	58	59	60
	61	62	63	64	65	66														
Jeremiah	1	2	3	4	5	6	7	8	9	10	11	12	13	14	15	16	17	18	19	20
	21	22	23	24	25	26	27	28	29	30	31	32	33	34	35	36	37	38	39	40
	41	42	43	44	45	46	47	48	49	50	51	52								
Lamentations	1	2	3	4	5															
Ezekiel	1	2	3	4	5	6	7	8	9	10	11	12	13	14	15	16	17	18	19	20
	21	22	23	24	25	26	27	28	29	30	31	32	33	34	35	36	37	38	39	40
	41	42	43	44	45	46	47	48												
Daniel	1	2	3	4	5	6	7	8	9	10	11	12								
Hosea	1	2	3	4	5	6	7	8	9	10	11	12	13	14						
Joel	1	2	3																	
Amos	1	2	3	4	5	6	7	8	9											
Obadiah	1																			
Jonah	1	2	3	4																
Micah	1	2	3	4	5	6	7													
Nahum	1	2	3																	
Habakkuk	1	2	3																	
Zephaniah	1	2	3																	
Haggai	1	2																		
Zechariah	1	2	3	4	5	6	7	8	9	10	11	12	13	14						
Malachi	1	2	3	4																

New Testament

Book	1	2	3	4	5	6	7	8	9	10	11	12	13	14	15	16	17	18	19	20	21	22	23	24	25	26	27	28
Matthew	1	2	3	4	5	6	7	8	9	10	11	12	13	14	15	16	17	18	19	20	21	22	23	24	25	26	27	28
Mark	1	2	3	4	5	6	7	8	9	10	11	12	13	14	15	16												
Luke	1	2	3	4	5	6	7	8	9	10	11	12	13	14	15	16	17	18	19	20	21	22	23	24				
John	1	2	3	4	5	6	7	8	9	10	11	12	13	14	15	16	17	18	19	20	21							
Acts	1	2	3	4	5	6	7	8	9	10	11	12	13	14	15	16	17	18	19	20	21	22	23	24	25	26	27	28
Romans	1	2	3	4	5	6	7	8	9	10	11	12	13	14	15	16												
1 Corinthians	1	2	3	4	5	6	7	8	9	10	11	12	13	14	15	16												
2 Corinthians	1	2	3	4	5	6	7	8	9	10	11	12	13															
Galatians	1	2	3	4	5	6																						
Ephesians	1	2	3	4	5	6																						
Philippians	1	2	3	4																								
Colossians	1	2	3	4																								
1Thessalonians	1	2	3	4	5																							
2Thessalonians	1	2	3																									
1 Timothy	1	2	3	4	5	6																						
2 Timothy	1	2	3	4																								
Titus	1	2	3																									
Philemon	1																											
Hebrews	1	2	3	4	5	6	7	8	9	10	11	12	13															
James	1	2	3	4	5																							
1 Peter	1	2	3	4	5																							
2 Peter	1	2	3																									
1 John	1	2	3	4	5																							
2 John	1																											
3 John	1																											
Jude	1																											
Revelation	1	2	3	4	5	6	7	8	9	10	11	12	13	14	15	16	17	18	19	20	21	22						

Read the Bible Through in a Year

Here is a schedule to read the Bible through in a year. The chapters are arranged in chronological order, so you read them somewhat in order of the time they describe. For example, when you read the Psalms of David, you may also read chapters from 1 and 2 Samuel and 1 Kings that record events surrounding the writing of the Psalms. And the writings of the prophets appear closer to their historical context

Jan 1.............................Genesis 1,2
Jan 2.............................Genesis 3-5
Jan 3.............................Genesis 6-9
Jan 4.........................Genesis 10,11
Jan 5........................Genesis 12-15
Jan 6........................Genesis 16-19
Jan 7........................Genesis 20-22
Jan 8........................Genesis 23-26
Jan 9........................Genesis 27-29
Jan 10......................Genesis 30-32
Jan 11......................Genesis 33-36
Jan 12......................Genesis 37-39
Jan 13......................Genesis 40-42
Jan 14......................Genesis 43-46
Jan 15......................Genesis 47-50
Jan 16...............................Job 1-4
Jan 17...............................Job 5-7
Jan 18.............................Job 8-10
Jan 19...........................Job 11-13
Jan 20...........................Job 14-17
Jan 21...........................Job 18-20
Jan 22...........................Job 21-24
Jan 23...........................Job 25-27
Jan 24...........................Job 28-31
Jan 25...........................Job 32-34
Jan 26...........................Job 35-37
Jan 27...........................Job 38-42
Jan 28.......................Exodus 1-4
Jan 29.......................Exodus 5-7
Jan 30.......................Exodus 8-10

Jan 31.....................Exodus 11-13
Feb 1.......................Exodus 14-17
Feb 2.......................Exodus 18-20
Feb 3.......................Exodus 21-24
Feb 4.......................Exodus 25-27
Feb 5.......................Exodus 28-31
Feb 6.......................Exodus 32-34
Feb 7.......................Exodus 35-37
Feb 8.......................Exodus 38-40
Feb 9........................Leviticus 1-4
Feb 10......................Leviticus 5–7
Feb 11....................Leviticus 8-10
Feb 12...................Leviticus 11-13
Feb 13...................Leviticus 14-16
Feb 14...................Leviticus 17-19
Feb 15....Leviticus 20-22, Psalm 95
Feb 16...................Leviticus 23-27
Feb 17......................Numbers 1-3
Feb 18......................Numbers 4-6
Feb 19....................Numbers 7-10
Feb 20.................Numbers 11-12;
                                  Psalm 90
Feb 21...Psalm 91; Numbers 13-14
Feb 22...................Numbers 15-17
Feb 23.................Numbers 18-20
Feb 24...............Numbers 21-24
Feb 25..................Numbers 25-27
Feb 26.................Numbers 28-30
Feb 27..................Numbers 31-33
Feb 28.................Numbers 34-36

Mar 1................Deuteronomy 1-3
Mar 2................Deuteronomy 4-6
Mar 3................Deuteronomy 7-9
Mar 4............Deuteronomy 10-12
Mar 5............Deuteronomy 13-16
Mar 6............Deuteronomy 17-19
Mar 7............Deuteronomy 20-22
Mar 8............Deuteronomy 23-25
Mar 9............Deuteronomy 26-28
Mar 10..........Deuteronomy 29-31
Mar 11..........Deuteronomy 32-34
Mar 12........................Joshua 1-3
Mar 13........................Joshua 4-6
Mar 14........................Joshua 7-9
Mar 15......................Joshua 10-12
Mar 16......................Joshua 13-15
Mar 17......................Joshua 16-18
Mar 18......................Joshua 19-21
Mar 19......................Joshua 22-24
Mar 20..........................Judges 1-4
Mar 21..........................Judges 5-8
Mar 22........................Judges 9-12
Mar 23......................Judges 13-15
Mar 24......................Judges 16-18
Mar 25......................Judges 19-21
Mar 26............................Ruth 1-4
Mar 27......................1 Samuel 1-4
Mar 28......................1 Samuel 5–8
Mar 29....................1 Samuel 9-12
Mar 30..................1 Samuel 13-16
Mar 31....1 Samuel 17–18; Psalm 23
Apr 1................1 Samuel 19:1-18;
Psalms 11,59
Apr 2.....1 Samuel 19:19-24;20–21;
Psalms 56,142
Apr 3........................1 Samuel 22;
Psalms 17, 34, 35
Apr 4................Psalms 52,109,140
Apr 5.......Psalms 31,64; 1 Samuel 23
Apr 6....Psalms 54,22; 1 Samuel 24
Apr 7...................Psalms 63,12,57
Apr 8....Psalms 58, 120; 1 Samuel 25

Apr 9....Psalm 141; 1 Samuel 26,27
Apr 10...................1 Samuel 28-30
Apr 11.....1 Samuel 31; 2 Samuel 1,2
Apr 12....Psalm 101; 2 Samuel 3–4
Apr 13........................2 Samuel 5;
Psalm 139; 2 Samuel 6
Apr 14......................Psalms 78,96
Apr 15..................Psalms 15,24,68
Apr 16...................Psalms 132,133
Apr 17...................Psalms 106, 105
Apr 18.....2 Samuel 7; Psalms 16,2
Apr 19.........................Psalm 110;
2 Samuel 8; Psalms 97,98
Apr 20............Psalms 108,117,118
Apr 21....................Psalms 60,9,20
Apr 22....................2 Samuel 9-11
Apr 23....2 Samuel 12; Psalms 6,32
Apr 24...........Psalms 33,38,39,21
Apr 25..................Psalms 40,41,51
Apr 26.................Psalms 103,104;
2 Samuel 13
Apr 27....Psalm 55; 2 Samuel 14,15
Apr 28......................2 Samuel 16;
Psalm 7; 2 Samuel 17
Apr 29.....................Psalms 3,4,42
Apr 30.....................Psalms 43,5,8
May 1..................Psalms 28,61,62
May 2..................Psalms 69-71,86
May 3.........................Psalms 143,
2 Samuel 18,19
May 4..............Psalms 122, 26, 27
May 5...Psalms 141, 65; 2 Samuel 20
May 6........................2 Samuel 21;
Psalms 29,30
May 7....................Psalms 131, 18;
2 Samuel 22-24; 1 Kings 1
May 8...................Psalms 72, 145;
1 Kings 2
May 9.........................1 Kings 3-5
May 10....Psalms 99,100, 127, 128
May 11......................Proverbs 1-4
May 12......................Proverbs 5-7

May 13.....................Proverbs 8-11	Jun 21.............................Isaiah 7-9
May 14.....................Proverbs 12-15	Jun 22.........................Isaiah 10-13
May 15.....................Proverbs 16-19	Jun 23.........................Isaiah 14-17
May 16.....................Proverbs 20-23	Jun 24.........................Isaiah 18-21
May 17.....................Proverbs 24-27	Jun 25.........................Isaiah 22-25
May 18.....................Proverbs 28-30	Jun 26.........................Isaiah 26-28
May 19........................Proverbs 31;	Jun 27.........................Isaiah 29-30
Ecclesiastes 1,2	Jun 28.........................Isaiah 31-33
May 20..................Ecclesiastes 3-5	Jun 29.........................Isaiah 34-36
May 21..................Ecclesiastes 6-8	Jun 30.........................Isaiah 37-39
May 22.................Ecclesiastes 9-11	Jul 1.............................Isaiah 40-42
May 23....Ecclesiastes 12; Song 1,2	Jul 2.............................Isaiah 43-45
May 24............................Song 3-5	Jul 3.............................Isaiah 46-48
May 25............................Song 6-8	Jul 4.............................Isaiah 49-51
May 26.......................1 Kings 6-8	Jul 5.............................Isaiah 52-54
May 27.......................1 Kings 9-11	Jul 6.............................Isaiah 55-57
May 28....................1 Kings 12-14	Jul 7.............................Isaiah 58-60
May 29....................1 Kings 15-17	Jul 8.............................Isaiah 61-63
May 30....................1 Kings 18-20	Jul 9.............................Isaiah 64-66
May 31....1 Kings 21,22; 2 Kings 1	Jul 10...............................Micah 1-4
Jun 1.............................2 Kings 2-4	Jul 11...............................Micah 5-7
Jun 2.............................2 Kings 5-7	Jul 12.............................Nahum 1-3
Jun 3..........................2 Kings 8-10	Jul 13.........................2 Kings 20,21
Jun 4...................2 Kings 11-14:20	Jul 14.........................Zephaniah 1-3
Jun 5..................................Joel 1-3	Jul 15.......................Habakkuk 1-3
Jun 6..................2 Kings 14:21-25;	Jul 16......................2 Kings 22-23;
Jonah 1-4	Psalm 74
Jun 7....2 Kings 14:26-29; Amos 1-3	Jul 17.......................Psalms 79, 94;
Jun 8...............................Amos 4-6	2 Kings 24:1-16
Jun 9...............................Amos 7-9	Jul 18...........................Psalm 88;
Jun 10.....................2 Kings 15-17	2 Kings 24:17-20, 25
Jun 11..............................Hosea 1-4	Jul 19..........Obadiah; Jeremiah 1,2
Jun 12..............................Hosea 5-7	Jul 20.........................Jeremiah 3-5
Jun 13.............................Hosea 8-10	Jul 21.........................Jeremiah 6-8
Jun 14..........................Hosea 11-14	Jul 22.......................Jeremiah 9-12
Jun 15...........2 Kings 18; Psalm 44	Jul 23....Jeremiah 13; Psalms 13,14
Jun 16....2 Kings 19:1-34; Psalm 73	Jul 24...................Psalms 36,37,49
Jun 17................2 Kings 19:35-37;	Jul 25...................Psalms 53,77,89
Psalms 92, 93	Jul 26.............................Psalm 123
Jun 18.................Psalms 46, 75, 76	Jul 27.....................Psalms 25,50,67
Jun 19...............................Isaiah 1-3	Jul 28.....................Psalms 102,130
Jun 20...............................Isaiah 4-6	Jul 29.......................Jeremiah 14-16

Jul 30....................Jeremiah 17-20
Jul 31....................Jeremiah 21-23
Aug 1....................Jeremiah 24-26
Aug 2....................Jeremiah 27-29
Aug 3....................Jeremiah 30-32
Aug 4....................Jeremiah 33-36
Aug 5....................Jeremiah 37-39
Aug 6....................Jeremiah 40-42
Aug 7....................Jeremiah 43-46
Aug 8....................Jeremiah 47-49
Aug 9....................Jeremiah 50-52
Aug 10...............Lamentations 1-5
Aug 11..............1 Chronicles 1-3
Aug 12..............1 Chronicles 4-6
Aug 13..............1 Chronicles 7-9
Aug 14.............1 Chronicles 10-13
Aug 15.............1 Chronicles 14-16
Aug 16.............1 Chronicles 17-19
Aug 17.............1 Chronicles 20-23
Aug 18.............1 Chronicles 24-26
Aug 19.............1 Chronicles 27-29
Aug 20.................2 Chronicles 1-3
Aug 21.................2 Chronicles 4-6
Aug 22.................2 Chronicles 7-9
Aug 23..............2 Chronicles 10-13
Aug 24..............2 Chronicles 14-16
Aug 25..............2 Chronicles 17-19
Aug 26...........................Psalm 82;
2 Chronicles 20; Psalm 83
Aug 27.............Psalms 47, 48, 115
Aug 28.............2 Chronicles 21-24
Aug 29.............2 Chronicles 25-27
Aug 30...........2 Chronicles 28–29;
Psalm 80
Aug 31.............2 Chronicles 30-32
Sep 1.................2 Chronicles 33-36
Sep 2..........................Ezekiel 1-3
Sep 3..........................Ezekiel 4-7
Sep 4..........................Ezekiel 8-11
Sep 5..........................Ezekiel 12-14
Sep 6..........................Ezekiel 15-18
Sep 7..........................Ezekiel 19-21

Sep 8........................Ezekiel 22-24
Sep 9........................Ezekiel 25-27
Sep 10......................Ezekiel 28-30
Sep 11......................Ezekiel 31-33
Sep 12......................Ezekiel 34-36
Sep 13......................Ezekiel 37-39
Sep 14......................Ezekiel 40-42
Sep 15......................Ezekiel 43-45
Sep 16......................Ezekiel 46-48
Sep 17..........................Daniel 1-3
Sep 18..........................Daniel 4-6
Sep 19..........................Daniel 7-9
Sep 20......................Daniel 10-12
Sep 21..Ezra 1; Psalms 85,126, 137
Sep 22..........Ezra 2; Psalms 1, 121
Sep 23...........................Psalm 119
Sep 24..........................Ezra 3:1-7;
Psalms 107,111
Sep 25..........Psalms 112, 113, 114
Sep 26.......................Ezra 3:8-13;
Psalms   66,84,116
Sep 27.................Psalms 125,129;
Ezra 4; Haggai 1,2
Sep 28......................Zechariah 1-3
Sep 29......................Zechariah 4-6
Sep 30....................Zechariah 7-10
Oct 1....................Zechariah 11-14
Oct 2.......................Ezra 5, 6:1-15;
Psalm 138
Oct 3........................Ezra 6:16-22;
Psalms 81, 134
Oct 4..............Psalms 135,136,146
Oct 5................Psalm 87; Ezra 7-8
Oct 6.............Ezra 9,10; Esther 1,2
Oct 7.......................Psalms 10,45;
Esther 3, 4:1-9
Oct 8..............Esther 4:10-17; 5-7
Oct 9......................Esther 8-10;
Psalm 124
Oct 10...................Nehemiah 1-3
Oct 11..................Psalms 147-149
Oct 12..................Nehemiah 4-6

Oct 13..................Psalms 150, 19;
Nehemiah 7

Oct 14.................Nehemiah 8-10

Oct 15.................Nehemiah 11-13

Oct 16.......................Malachi 1-4

Oct 17.....................Matthew 1-4

Oct 18.....................Matthew 5-7

Oct 19.....................Matthew 8-11

Oct 20...................Matthew 12-15

Oct 21...................Matthew 16-19

Oct 22...................Matthew 20-22

Oct 23...................Matthew 23-25

Oct 24...................Matthew 26-28

Oct 25..........................Mark 1-3

Oct 26..........................Mark 4-6

Oct 27.........................Mark 7-10

Oct 28........................Mark 11-13

Oct 29........................Mark 14-16

Oct 30............................Luke 1-4

Oct 31............................Luke 5-8

Nov 1............................Luke 9-12

Nov 2...........................Luke 13-16

Nov 3...........................Luke 17-20

Nov 4...........................Luke 21-24

Nov 5...............................John 1-4

Nov 6...............................John 5-8

Nov 7..............................John 9-12

Nov 8...........................John 13-16

Nov 9...........................John 17-21

Nov 10.............................Acts 1-3

Nov 11.............................Acts 4-6

Nov 12.............................Acts 7-9

Nov 13.........................Acts 10-14

Nov 14...........................James 1–2

Nov 15...........................James 3-5

Nov 16.....................Galatians 1-3

Nov 17.....................Galatians 4-6

Nov 18...................Acts 15-18:11

Nov 19............1 Thessalonians 1-5

Nov 20..........2 Thessalonians 1-3;
Acts 18:12-19:10

Nov 21...............1 Corinthians 1-4

Nov 22...............1 Corinthians 5-8

Nov 23.............1 Corinthians 9-12

Nov 24...........1 Corinthians 13-16

Nov 25.................Acts 19:11-20:1;
2 Corinthians 1-3

Nov 26.............2 Corinthians 4-6

Nov 27.............2 Corinthians 7-9

Nov 28.........2 Corinthians 10-13;
Acts 20:2

Nov 29........................Romans 1-4

Nov 30........................Romans 5-6

Dec 1..........................Romans 7-9

Dec 2.......................Romans 10-12

Dec 3.......................Romans 13-16

Dec 4.............................Acts 20-22

Dec 5.............................Acts 23-25

Dec 6.............................Acts 26-28

Dec 7.......................Ephesians 1-3

Dec 8.......................Ephesians 4-6

Dec 9....................Philippians 1-4

Dec 10....................Colossians 1-4

Dec 11.......................Hebrews 1-4

Dec 12.......................Hebrews 5-7

Dec 13.....................Hebrews 8-10

Dec 14..................Hebrews 11-13

Dec 15..........Philemon; 1 Peter 1,2

Dec 16............................1 Peter 3-5

Dec 17............................2 Peter 1-3

Dec 18.....................1 Timothy 1-3

Dec 19.....................1 Timothy 4-6

Dec 20.............................Titus 1-3

Dec 21.....................2 Timothy 1-4

Dec 22...........................1 John 1,2

Dec 23...........................1 John 3-5

Dec 24..........2 John; 3 John; Jude

Dec 25....................Revelation 1-3

Dec 26....................Revelation 4-6

Dec 27....................Revelation 7-9

Dec 28.................Revelation 10-12

Dec 29.................Revelation 13-15

Dec 30.................Revelation 16-18

Dec 31.................Revelation 19-22

Verses to Memorize

Goal: To understand your position in Christ as a result of defending your faith.

1. Result of sin .... Romans 6:23
2. Salvation is a free gift (can't be earned) .... Ephesians 2:8–9
3. All are sinners .... Romans 3:23
4. Who God is (Jesus didn't "become" a God) .... John 1:1
5. Christ is the only way to heaven (not many ways to heaven) .... John 14:6
6. Description of Faith (good works follow salvation) ..... James 2:17–18
7. Assurance of salvation (won't lose it) .... John 10:27–28
8. All should be baptized after salvation (the Trinity) ...... Matthew 28:19
9. Make disciples of all nations (evangelize) .... Matthew 28:20
10. The Bible is God's Word (total truth) .... 2 Timothy 3:16–17
11. There is a God (nature shows there is a God) .... Psalm 19:1
12. Jesus dies for our sins .... Isaiah 53:5–6
13. God is love .... John 3:16
14. Jesus was born of a virgin .... Isaiah 7:14
15. We can go directly to God .... 1 Timothy 2:5
16. The Holy Spirit is inside every Christian .... Romans 8:9
17. Sin comes through one person. Life does too .... Romans 5:12
18. God wants commitment .... Romans 12:1
19. Separation from the world .... Romans 12:2
20. The devil is alive now .... 1 Peter 5:8
21. We're in a spiritual war .... Ephesians 6:12
22. Death is coming. Christ will return .... Hebrews 9:27–28
23. The Lord is returning .... 1 Thessalonians 4:16-17
24. Hell is our destination if our name is not in the book of life ....
.... Revelation 20:15
25. Church involvement .... Hebrews 10:25
26. Distinctive of communion .... John 13:14–15
27. Love not the world .... 1 John 2:15–17
28. Christ's ambassadors .... 2 Corinthians 5:20
29. Don't be yoked with unbelievers .... 2 Corinthians 6:14
30. Don't repay evil with evil .... 1 Peter 3:9
31. Don't be mastered by anything .... 1 Corinthians 6:12
32. Dealing with temptation .... 1 Corinthians 10:13
33. Example to youth .... 1 Timothy 4:12
34. Approved by God .... 2 Timothy 2:15

Scripture Memory Course

The following verses suggest a balance in Scripture memory. The verses selected are key verses to understand the foundations of the Christian Life and Christian Growth. Do not feel tied to this suggested list. It is only a tool to help you understand the importance of memorizing key verses.

Live the New Life

Christ the Center	2 Corinthians 5:17; Galatians 2:20
Obedience to Christ	Romans 12:1; John 14:21
The Word	2 Timothy 3:16; Joshua 1:8
Prayer	John 15:7; Philippians 4:6–7
Fellowship	Matthew 18:20; Hebrews 10:24
Witnessing	Matthew 4:19; Romans 1:16

Proclaim Christ

All Have Sinned	Romans 3:23; Isaiah 53:6
Sin's Penalty	Romans 6:23; Hebrews 9:27
Christ Paid the Penalty	Romans 5:8; 1 Peter 3:18
Salvation Not by Works	Ephesians 2:8–9; Titus 3:5
Must Receive Christ	John 1:12; Romans 10:13
Assurance of Salvation	1 John 5:13; John 5:24

Rely on God's Resources

His Spirit	1 Corinthians 3:16; 1 Corinthians 2:12
His Strength	Isaiah 41:10; Philippians 4:13
His Faithfulness	Lamentations 3:22; Numbers 23:19
His Peace	Isaiah 26:3; 1 Peter 5:7
His Provision	Romans 8:32; Philippians 4:19
His Help in Temptation	Hebrews 2:18; Psalm 119:9, 11; 2 Corinthians 10:13

Be Christ's Disciple

Put Christ First   Matthew 6:33; Luke 9:23
Separate from the World 1 John 2:15–16; Romans 12:2
Be Steadfast   1 Corinthians 15:58; Hebrews 12:3
Serve Others   Mark 10:45; 2 Corinthians 4:5
Give Generously   Proverbs 3:9–10; 2 Corinthians 9:6–7
Develop World Vision   Acts 1:8; Matthew 28:19–20

Grow in Christlikeness

Love   John 13:34–35; 1 John 3:18
Humility   Philippians 2:3-4; 1 Peter 5:5–6
Purity   Ephesians 5:3; 1 Peter 2:11
Honesty   Leviticus 19:11; Acts 24:16
Faith   Hebrews 11:6; Romans 4:20–21
Good Works   Galatians 6:9–10; Matthew 5:16

Chapter 6

The Habit of Prayer

There is public prayer and there is private prayer. My ABS partner and I are sitting in a Dunkin' Donuts, a Starbucks, a Panera Bread, or even a McDonalds. After encouraging one another, asking each other the hard questions, and discussing what we have been studying, we bow our heads and pray for one another. It's not uncommon for someone to approach us and make a comment about our courage to pray in a public setting. Honestly, I think almost every time this occurs, the person is a believer in Jesus Christ.

Then there is the lunch appointment in a very high-class restaurant, where it is common for the business community to enjoy a fine meal while trying to land the perfect business deal. The person I am with may or may not be a believer; I am not sure. The time has come to pray to give thanks before my meal. I cower and opt for the "drop the napkin and offer up a quick prayer of thanks" option, while picking up the napkin. Whew…no one noticed.

Everyone knows I am a Christian, and I am involved in the Chamber of Commerce. I attend many of the fundraisers for groups like the YMCA. I attend my kids' high school sports banquets. Each of these groups invites me to give the invocation. That sounds important. How will I talk to God? Will I talk to a "generic" God? Will I script out my prayer and comments to impress those who hear it?

At the beginning of the day, my wife and our four children are all running around the house frantically getting ready for work and for school. All of us have incredibly busy schedules. We are going in different directions. We need to take showers; we need to eat breakfast to ensure the energy required to sustain us throughout the course of the day. We all rush out the door. So often we neglect to gather together and ask God for His direction and opportunities that day. In essence we walk out the door and let God know we can handle this day.

All that is true until a crisis hits. Then we pull out the "prayer card." That is the card I have come to rely on. After all it's prayer, and when I need God, why would I not go to Him? That says a whole lot about my life. I have not taken the time to understand prayer. I have not made prayer a daily habit in my life. I use prayer like a tool and too often this tool stays in the bottom of my toolbox. I have become too self-sufficient. I have not understood how much I really need God in my daily life.

Let's learn why we pray and why we don't. Let's learn how to make prayer a daily discipline in our lives that will be the foundation of our spiritual fitness. No one can develop ABS of Faith without this exercise.

We've all noticed it. Sometimes in a group prayer setting someone goes on and on with a lot of "stuff." We can tell the primary desire seems to be to impress other people. But prayer is not about impressing others or even impressing God. We don't pray what we think God or other people want to hear. God already knows our hearts and our thoughts. We're not fooling Him. We are just to tell Him what's on our hearts. Jesus cautioned, *When you pray, do not be like the hypocrites, for they love to pray standing in the synagogues and on the street corners to be seen by men* (Matt. 6:5).

Romans 12:12 says, *Be glad for all God is planning for you. Be patient in trouble, and prayerful always* (TLB).

Approaching Prayer with the Right Attitude

The first attitude we need as we pray is honesty, transparency, to be real. The Pharisees tried to impress other people. They stood on street corners, raised their hands and their faces to the sky and carried on in a very public way, to impress others. Scripture says we are not to be like the Pharisees. Don't try to impress people.

The second attitude is to be relaxed. *But when you pray, go into your room, close the door and pray to your Father who is unseen. Then your Father, who sees what is done in secret, will reward you* (Matt. 6:6). We need to go someplace where we can be alone with God, where we can be quiet without distractions and concentrate.

Third, be revealing. *Don't recite the same prayer over and over as the heathen do, who think prayers are answered only by repeating them again and again. Remember, your Father knows exactly what you need even before you ask Him!* (Matt. 6:7–8 TLB). When we talk to the Lord, we just talk. That's what prayer is. It's a conversation between two people who love each other. When I need something from my wife, I don't come to her and say, "O Thou most honored of women, I need some money for golf if thou wilt bless it to me." No, I just say, "Hey! I need some money for golf." I just talk to her because we have a love relationship. When we come to God, we just tell Him what's really on our hearts.

Using the Model Jesus Gave Us

In the model prayer that we refer to as the Lord's Prayer, Jesus said, *This then, is how you should pray* (Matt. 6:9). He didn't say, "This is what you should pray." In this prayer, recorded in Matthew 6:9–15, Jesus gives us an illustration of elements we should include in prayer, not a specific prayer to pray.

Praise is the beginning of that prayer. We begin by expressing our love to God. Jesus prayed, *Our Father in heaven, /*

hallowed be your name (v. 9*)*. When we pray, we should begin by expressing our love to God. We start by saying to Him, "Lord, I want to focus on You." If we come to prayer focusing on ourselves and our own needs first, we'll leave prayer more depressed and frustrated than when we began. But if we come with the attitude of focusing on God—what we can see of Him, what we can learn of Him, and what He can show us—then we're going to have the right perspective.

There are two kinds of praise. One is adoration, which is praising God for who He is, His character. The other is thanksgiving, praising God for what He has done or His deeds. We should include both when we come before the Lord—thanking Him for who He is and thanking Him for what He has done. *Enter his gates with thanksgiving and his courts with praise; give thanks to him and praise his name* (Psalm 100:4).

The next part of the model prayer is purpose: I commit myself to God's purpose and will for my life. *Your kingdom come, / your will be done on earth as it is in heaven* (Matthew 6:10) is an acknowledgment that God is God and I am not. At this time in prayer I want to pray for God's will to be done in my family, in my church, among my friends, and in my city. This is where I open myself to the Lord and say, "Just do whatever You need to do in my life."

I think the seven most profound words of Scripture are spoken by the mother of Jesus, at the first miracle He performed at the wedding in Cana. The wine had run out and Jesus had told them what to do about it, but it did not make sense to them. So they asked His mother what she thought. She replied, "Whatever He says to you, do it" (John 2:5 NASB). Nike has made millions off that line—"Just Do It," but it was Mary who first said it. That's what this time is about in prayer. "God, You do whatever You need to do in my life."

Claim Romans 12:2 (NLT) which says, *Don't copy the behavior and customs of this world, but let God transform you into a new person by changing the way you think. Then you will know what God wants you to do, and you will know how good and pleasing and perfect his will really is.* First I come to praise the Lord for who He is and what He has done. Then I commit myself by saying, "You do whatever You need to do in my life, because You're God."

After we commit ourselves to God's purpose, we pray for His provision. This is where I ask God to provide for my needs. What needs do I pray about? I pray about all of them. There is nothing too great for God's power to take care of and nothing too insignificant for His concern. So I pray about all my needs. Paul writes, *And this same God who takes care of me will supply all your needs from his glorious riches, which have been given to us in Christ Jesus* (Philippians 4:19 NLT). In Romans he tells us, *Since God did not spare even his own Son but gave him up for us all, won't God, who gave us Christ, also give us everything else?* (Rom. 8:32 NLT). Saving us is the greatest thing God ever did. So when we ask Him to fill our needs, it's a piece of cake in comparison.

James states, *You do not have, because you do not ask God* (James 4:2). Wishing and hoping for something is not the same as specifically asking for it. When we have a need, we can ask God for it. And we can be specific. I write down my requests with the promise that I'm claiming from the Bible, and I expect God to answer.

Next in this prayer is the cry for pardon. I confess my sin and ask God to forgive and cleanse me from all my sin. This part of the Lord's Prayer says, *Forgive us our debts* (v. 12).

Four Steps to Forgiveness

We ask the Holy Spirit to reveal our sin.

He's so good to do that. When I come to Him with an honest heart, He will reveal the sin in my life. We should pray with the psalmist, *Search me, O God, and know my heart; test me and know my thoughts. Point out anything in me that offends you, and*

lead me along the path of everlasting life (Psalm 139:23–24 NLT).
I ask the Holy Spirit to reveal the sin in me.

We confess each sin specifically.

Sometimes we like to get away with confession of sin by just
saying, "Forgive all my sins." But we committed those sins individually. That means we had better ask forgiveness for those
sins individually. Proverbs 28:13 reminds us that *people who
cover over their sins will not prosper. But if they confess and forsake
them, they will receive mercy* (NLT).

We make restitution to others when necessary.

In Matthew 5:23–24 we read, *"So if you are standing before the
altar in the Temple, offering a sacrifice to God, and you suddenly
remember that someone has something against you, / leave your
sacrifice there beside the altar. Go and be reconciled to that person.
Then come and offer your sacrifice to God* (NLT). When God
reveals to us something that we have done to someone else, we
need to make restitution and get it off our conscience.

By faith, we accept God's forgiveness.

We are given the assurance that *if we confess our sins, he is faithful and just and will forgive us our sins and purify us from all
unrighteousness* (1 John 1:9). God can forgive all sin. He can
wipe out the guilt. We must realize we don't have to live with
guilt. It can be forgiven; the slate can be wiped clean.

In this prayer I see how I can pray for other people. The
Lord's Prayer continues, *And forgive us our sins, just as we have
forgiven those who have sinned against us* ((Matt. 6:12 NLT). Paul
urged Timothy, *First of all, to pray for all people. As you make
your requests, plead for God's mercy upon them, and give thanks*
(1 Tim. 2:1 NLT). Remember that God is working in the lives
of people we pray for even when we can't see it.

If we've been praying for a long time for someone and we
don't see any evidence of change, we may want to give up.
"Forget it," we want to say. "Prayer doesn't really work. There's

no point in it. I don't know why I'm wasting my breath." Scripture says we should pray much and plead for God's mercy. We are to give thanks for all He is going to do for him or her. We can be assured that whoever it is we're praying for, God is working in that person even though we can't see the evidence of it. We are never given permission to stop praying for someone. We are to pray until God has changed us, changed the situation, or changed the person. So we keep praying.

And, in the conclusion of the model prayer, we ask God for spiritual protection: *And lead us not into temptation / but deliver us from the evil one* (Matt. 6:13). We face a spiritual battle every day, and Satan wants to defeat us through temptation and fear. If we start every day without praying for God's protection, we are walking into battle unprotected. We are walking onto the battlefield without the spiritual armor we're to put on (Eph. 6:11-18). We can ask God to make us aware of the evil in this world. If we're unaware of it, we may be caught by it. We can be trapped before we even know what's going on. But if we ask the Lord to make us aware of evil and tempting situations, He will help us fight them. The apostle John tells us, *The Spirit who lives in you is greater than the spirit who lives in the world* (1 John 4:4 NLT). We don't have to be afraid. The Spirit who is in us is more powerful than the spirit who is in the world.

The aids on the following pages will assist you in developing an active prayer life. Use these helps; watch what God does in your life as you grow in prayer. I am confident that as you invest and discipline yourself in these spiritual exercises you will develop the ABS of Faith that will leave you standing in the presence of our Lord, hearing the wonderful words, *Well done, good and faithful slave; you were faithful with a few things, I will put you in charge of many things; enter into the joy of your master* (Matt. 25:23 NASB).

How to Pray Effectively in Your Quiet Time

The Hand Of Prayer

There are five major types of prayer.

1. The finger (thumb) of confession. 1 John 1:9
2. The index finger of petition. Matthew 6:11
3. The middle finger of intercession. 1 Timothy 2:1–4; John 17
4. The ring finger of praise. 1 Chronicles 29:10–13
5. The little finger of thanksgiving. 1 Thessalonians 5:18; Ephesians 5:20

The fingers are to aid memory and are not related to the value of the kinds of prayer.

Why Pray Daily To God?

1. To glorify God. John 14:13
2. For victory over temptation. Matthew 26:41, 6:13
3. To love God we must know Him; through prayer we come to know Him and grow in love. Matthew 22:37
4. We have been called to fellowship with Christ. 1 Corinthians 1:9
5. We are commanded to pray. 1 Thessalonians 5:17
6. For self-analysis. Psalm 139:23–24
7. God *wants* to fellowship with us! John 4:23
8. To experience God's grace in our lives. Hebrews 4:15–16
9. To conform our will to His. Matthew 6:10
10. To receive God's blessings. James 4:2
11. To keep from sinning. 1 Samuel 12:23
12. To have fullness of joy. John 16:24
13. To come close to God. James 4:8
14. To be forgiven. 1 John 1:9
15. For laborers for the ministry. Matthew 9:36–37

Three Essentials For An Effective Quiet Time
Daniel 6:10–11

1. You must have a definite *place.*

   It should be quiet; a regular place where you feel at home with the Lord. It might be back of a house, in a room, auto, or even walking outside.

2. You must have a definite *time.*

   To give God 10 minutes more than you do, work back to when you get up. You need to get up 10 minutes earlier. The secret to getting up is going to bed! Make an *appointment* with God for a specific time, preferably in the mornings before you hit the pressures of the day.

   If you have difficulty waking up, take a cold shower. Commitment more than anything else makes the difference in victory here. Proverbs 20:4

   Ruth Paxson, missionary to China in the early part of the 20th century, said, *Prayer works, prayer is work, prayer leads to work.* Since prayer is work, it should be scheduled like any other work, with a specific time.

3. You must have definite *content* for prayer.

   - Pray aloud rather than silently; this helps concentration and prepares you to pray effectively in public.

   - Pray a verse back to God; in your quiet time first read the Scriptures, then go to prayer, meditating on what you have just read. Take ideas and verses and echo them back to the Lord.

   - Be specific; generality kills prayer. Use as many kinds of prayer as you can.

- Use a map of the world for intercession; buy a map of your state or city, and specifically pray through the streets or towns asking God to move in specific ways in an area of the world, your state, and your local city or town.

- List requests on a *prayer possibilities* sheet. Write in answers; keep a notebook of answered prayer requests. They will grow. There are many ways to organize praying on a daily basis. The Spirit wants to lead us in prayer. Organizing requests is valuable. Here is one way:

Sunday: **People:** Relatives, Timothys, church workers, pastor, teachers.

Monday: **Possibilities:** Your goals, vision plans, ideas from God. "You are coming to a King, great petitions with you bring; for His grace and power are such, no one can ever ask too much."[1]

Tuesday: **Places:** Countries and missionaries around the world; pray for those in authority; laborers needed in your church, on the mission fields; everywhere.

Wednesday:**Prospects:** Evangelistic opportunities; pray for people by name in your neighborhood, where you work, your school, clubs, recreation contacts, church prospects.

Thursday: **Production:** Your own personal immediate goals and job; pray through all the people and possibilities where you work or serve. Ask God how you can better multiply your life for His glory.

---

[1] Hymn, "Come My Soul, Thy Suit Prepare," by John Newton (1725-1807).

Friday: **Power:** Dare to ask the Lord for His supernatural working in the lives of people who are apparently homeless. Claim a verse God brings to your heart for these people. Meditate on the ministry of the Holy Spirit to do the impossible in us.

Saturday: **Personal:** Your family needs, home, children, wife or husband. Ask God for a specific verse you can apply in your life for to those you love and are with daily. Psalm 139:23–24; Psalm 119:59–60. Be open for God to reveal sin, root out attitudes that are not of Christ. Pray one of the prayers of Paul for each family member.

Prayer Guide 1
Character Traits of God

Character Trait	**Scripture**
Faithful	2 Corinthians 1:20
Righteous	2 Timothy 4:8
The Light	John 8:12

Prayer Guide 2

The Names of God

Did you know that God has several names? They are all in the Bible and each name describes a facet of His character. You can take each of these eight names and focus individually on what God is really like. Pray the names of God as affirmations of praise.

Eight Hebrew Names of God—Declare Who God Is

Jehovah-Shammah—"God is Present with me" (Ezekiel 48:35)
You are here. I am never alone.

Jehovah-Rohi—"God is my Shepherd" (Psalm 23:1)
You lead me and feed me and protect me.

Jehovah-Jireh—"God is my Provider" (Genesis 22:14)
You see what I need before I even ask.

Jehovah-Rophe—"God is my Healer" (Exodus 15:26)
You can heal my body, emotions, and relationships.

Jehovah-Tsidkenu—"God is my Righteousness" (Jeremiah 23:6)
You accept me and forgive me because of Jesus.

Jehovah-M'Kiddish—"God is my Sanctification" (Leviticus 20:8)
You make me holy and like Jesus.

Jehovah-Shalom—"God is my Peace" (Judges 6:24)
You give me peace in spite of circumstances.

Jehovah-Nissi—"God is my Banner" (Exodus 17:15)
You are my victory in conflict and confrontation.

Think on the implications of these names and you'll have plenty for which to praise God.

Prayer Guide 3

My Thanksgiving List

_____

_____

_____

_____

_____

_____

_____

_____

_____

_____

_____

_____

_____

_____

_____

_____

_____

_____

Prayer Guide 4
My Personal Requests

Date	Request	Promise	Date Answered

Prayer Guide 5
People I'm Praying for

Family

_____

_____

Christian Friends

_____

_____

Friends I'd like to see become Christians

_____

_____

Spiritual Leaders

_____

_____

Government Leaders

_____

_____

Others

_____

_____

30 Days, 30 Ways To Pray

Day 1:   Salvation (Isaiah 45:8; 2 Timothy 2:10)
Day 2:   Growth in Grace (2 Peter 3:18)
Day 3:   Love (Ephesians 5:2; Galatians 5:22)
Day 4:   Honesty and Integrity (Psalm 25:21)
Day 5:   Self Control (1 Thessalonians 5:6)
Day 6:   A Love for God's Word (Psalm 19:10)
Day 7:   Justice (Psalm 11:7; Micah 6:8)
Day 8:   Mercy (Luke 6:36)
Day 9:   Respect (for self, others, authority) (1 Peter 2:17)
Day 10:   Strong, Biblical Self-esteem (Ephesians 2:10)
Day 11:   Faithfulness (Proverbs 3:3)
Day 12:   A Passion for God (Psalm 63:8)
Day 13:   Responsibility (Galatians 6:5)
Day 14:   Kindness (1 Thessalonians 5:15)
Day 15:   Generosity (1 Timothy 6:18-19)
Day 16:   Peace, peaceability (Romans 14:19)
Day 17:   Hope (Romans 15:13)
Day 18:   Perseverance (Hebrews 12:1)
Day 19:   Humility (Titus 3:2)
Day 20:   Compassion (Colossians 3:12)
Day 21:   Prayerfulness (Ephesians 6:18)
Day 22:   Contentment (Phil. 4:12–13)
Day 23:   Faith (Luke 17:5-6; Hebrews 11:39–40)
Day 24:   A Servant Heart (Ephesians 6:7)
Day 25:   Purity (Psalm 51:10)
Day 26:   A Willingness and Ability to Work Hard (Colossians 3:23)
Day 27:   Self-discipline (Proverbs 1:3)
Day 28:   A Heart for Missions (Psalm 96:3)
Day 29:   Joy (1 Thessalonians 1:6)
Day 30:   Courage (Deuteronomy 31:6)

How To Spend An Hour With God – 1

Scripture Reading: Proverbs 5
    Note any areas of encouragement or conviction

Prayers of Adoration
Psalm 100:1–5, A psalm for giving thanks
    Shout for joy to the LORD, all the earth.
        Worship the LORD with gladness;
        come before him with joyful songs.
    Know that the LORD is God.
        It is he who made us, and we are his;
        we are his people, the sheep of his pasture.
    Enter his gates with thanksgiving
        and his courts with praise;
        give thanks to him and praise his name.
    For the LORD is good and his love endures forever;
    his faithfulness continues through all generations.

Pause here to express any thoughts of adoration.

Prayers for Forgiveness
Psalm 51:7–13
    Cleanse me with hyssop, and I will be clean;
        wash me, and I will be whiter than snow.
    Let me hear joy and gladness;
        let the bones you have crushed rejoice.
    Hide your face from my sins
        and blot out all my iniquity.
    Create in me a pure heart, O God,
        and renew a steadfast spirit within me.
    Do not cast me from your presence
        or take your Holy Spirit from me.
    Restore to me the joy of your salvation

and grant me a willing spirit, to sustain me.
Then I will teach transgressors your ways,
    and sinners will turn back to you.

Pause here to ask the Spirit of God to bring to your mind specific sins for which you need forgiveness, and confess them to the Lord.

Prayers for Renewal
Psalm 119:36–37
Turn my heart toward your statutes
    and not toward selfish gain.
Turn my eyes away from worthless things;
    preserve my life according to your word.
Hebrews 13:5
Keep your lives free from the love of money and be content with what you have, because God has said, "Never will I leave you; never will I forsake you."

Pause here for any additional prayers for renewal.

Prayers for Personal Needs
Spiritual Growth:
- Sensitivity to sin
- Greater love and commitment to the Lord
- Special concerns
- My activities for the day

Prayers for Others
The Church and Other Ministries:
- My local church
- Other churches
- Other Christian ministries
- Educational institutions
- Special concerns

Prayers of Affirmation

John 8:12

> When Jesus spoke again to the people, he said, "I am the light of the world. Whoever follows me will never walk in darkness, but will have the light of life."

John 6:35

> Then Jesus declared, "I am the bread of life. He who comes to me will never go hungry, and he who believes in me will never be thirsty."

John 4:14

> "...but whoever drinks the water I give him will never thirst. Indeed, the water I give him will become in him a spring of water welling up to eternal life."

Pause here to add any personal affirmations.

Prayers of Thanksgiving

Psalm 27:1

> The Lord is my light and my salvation--
>   whom shall I fear?
> The Lord is the stronghold of my life--
>   of whom shall I be afraid?

Malachi 4:2

> But for you who revere my name, the sun of righteousness will rise with healing in its wings. And you will go out and leap like calves released from the stall.

Pause here for any personal expressions of thanksgiving.

Closing Prayer

Hebrews 13:20-21

> May the God of peace, who through the blood of the eternal covenant brought back from the dead our Lord Jesus, that great Shepherd of the sheep, equip you with

everything good for doing his will, and may he work in us what is pleasing to him, through Jesus Christ, to whom be glory for ever and ever. Amen.

Memorize a verse of Scripture you need for your life.

How To Spend An Hour With God – 2

Scripture Reading: Read the book of Galatians
Note any areas of encouragement or conviction

Prayers of Adoration
Psalm 34:8,9:
Taste and see that the Lord is good;
blessed is the man who trusts in Him!
Fear the Lord, you His saints!
for those who fear him lack nothing.
Psalm 139:14:
I praise you because I am fearfully and wonderfully made;
your works are wonderful,
I know that full well.

Pause here to express any thoughts of adoration.

Prayers of Forgiveness
Psalm 32:1-5
Blessed is he
whose transgressions are forgiven,
whose sins are covered.
Blessed is the man
whose sin the Lord does not count against him
and in whose spirit is no deceit.
When I kept silent,
my bones wasted away
through my groaning all day long.
For day and night
your hand was heavy upon me;
my strength was sapped
as in the heat of summer.   Selah.

Then I acknowledged my sin to you,
    and did not cover up my iniquity.
I said, "I will confess
    my transgressions to the Lord"—
and you forgave
he guilt of my sin.   Selah.

Pause here to ask the Spirit of God to bring to your mind specific sins for which you need forgiveness, and confess them to the Lord.

Prayers for Renewal

Concerning stewardship, Your Word says, 1 Corinthians 4:2:
    It is required in stewards that one be found faithful.
And Luke 16:13:
    No servant can serve two masters. Either he will hate the one and love the other, or he will be devoted to the one and despise the other. You cannot serve God and money.
And Matthew 25:21:
    His master replied, "Well done, good and faithful servant! You have been faithful with a few things; I will put you in charge of many things. Come and share your master's happiness."
Pray: *may I be a faithful steward and enter into Your joy.*
Pause here for any additional prayers for renewal.

Prayer for Personal Needs

    Need for Wisdom:
- Wisdom for living life
- Developing an eternal perspective
- Renewal of my mind
- Special concerns
- My activities for this day

Prayers for Others
Family:
- My Immediate family
- My relatives
- The salvation of family members
- Special concerns

Prayers of Affirmation
2 Corinthians 5:17
Therefore, if anyone is in Christ, he is a new creation; the old has gone, the new has come!
Romans 6:11
In the same way, count yourselves dead to sin but alive to God In Christ Jesus.

Pause here to add any personal affirmations.

Prayers of Thanksgiving
Lord, thank You that You have made this promise:
Psalm 91:14-16:
"Because he loves Me, says the LORD, "I will rescue him;
I will protect him, be he acknowledges my name.
He will call upon me, and I will answer him;
I will be with him in trouble,
I will deliver him and honor him.
With long life I will satisfy him,
and show him My salvation.

Pause here for any personal expressions of thanksgiving.

Closing Prayer
Psalm 19:14
May the words of my mouth and the meditation of my heart
be pleasing in your sight,
O LORD, my Rock and my Redeemer.

Memorize a verse of Scripture you need for your life.

How To Spend An Hour With God – 3

Scripture Reading: Read John 14-17
Note any areas of which the Holy Spirit is convicting you.

Prayers of Adoration
1 Chronicles 29:10-13:
Praise be to you, O LORD,
God of our Father Israel,
from everlasting to everlasting.
Yours, O LORD, is the greatness and the power
And the glory and the majesty and the splendor,
for everything in heaven and earth is yours.
Yours, O LORD, is the kingdom;
you are exalted as head over all.
Wealth and honor come from you;
you are the ruler of all things.
In your hands are strength and power
to exalt and give strength to all.
Now, our God, we give you thanks,
and praise your glorious name.

Pause here to express any thoughts of adoration.

Prayers for Forgiveness
Thank You, Lord, that You have said:
Isaiah 43:25:
"I, even I, am He who blots out
your transgressions, for My own sake,
and remembers your sins no more."

Pause here to ask the Spirit of God to bring to your mind specific sins for which you need forgiveness, and confess them to the Lord.

Prayer for Renewal

Psalm 139:23,24:

> Search me, O God, and know my heart;
> Try me, and know my anxieties;
> And see if there is any wicked way in me,
> And lead me in the way everlasting.

Psalm 141:3,4:

> Set a guard over my mouth, O LORD;
> Keep watch over the door of my lips.
> Let not my heart be drawn to what is evil
> To take part in wicked deeds
> With men who are evildoers
> Let me not eat of their delicacies.

Psalm 119:133:

> Direct my steps according to your word;
> let no sin rule over me.

Pause here for any additional prayers for renewal.

Prayers for Personal Needs

Relationships with Others:

- Greater love and compassion for others
- Loved ones
- The lost
- Those in need
- Special concerns
- My activities for this day

Prayers for Others

Evangelism:

- Friends
- Neighbors
- Associates
- Special opportunities

Prayers of Affirmation

Romans 8:15:

> For you did not receive a spirit that makes you aslave
> again to fear, but you have received the Spirit of sonship.
> And by him cry, "Abba, Father."

Pause here to add any personal affirmations.

Prayers of Thanksgiving

Psalm 73:25,26:

> Whom have I in heaven but you?
>> And earth has nothing I desire besides you.
> My flesh and my heart may fail,
>> But God is the strength of my heart
>> and my portion forever.

Psalm 42:11:

> Why are you downcast, O my soul?
>> Why so disturbed within me?
> Put your hope in God,
>> for I will yet praise Him,
>> my Savior and my God.

Pause here for any personal expressions of thanksgiving.

Closing Prayer

Psalm 121:7,8:

> The LORD will keep you from all harm—
>> he will watch over your life;
> the LORD will watch over your coming and going
>> both now and forevermore.

Memorize a verse of Scripture you need for your life.

HOW TO SPEND AN HOUR WITH GOD – 4

Prayer for Forgiveness

Prayers for forgiveness acknowledge how we have fallen short of the glory and character of God. The more we grasp the holiness of God, the more we recognize the destructiveness and deceitfulness of sin (I John 1:5-22).

- Thank Him for His provision of forgiveness in Christ (Isaiah 53:5,6).
- Consider the following areas: your attitude, your tongue, your thoughts, and usage of time (Psalm 51:1-12).
- Rejoice in being forgiven! (Psalm 32:1-5).

Prayer of Adoration

Prayers of adoration are expressions of praise and worship to the LORD of all creation. With adoration, you exalt, honor, esteem, bless, and magnify the LORD as you reflect upon His goodness, grace, holiness, love, might, power, and dominion. In praise, you rejoice in God and express all that you have discovered Him to be. (Revelation 4:11)

- Pray Psalm 63:1-7 to God.
- Reflect on His love for man; for you. Consider His patience, grace, compassions, power, holiness, and sovereign . Thank Him for these things. Pray that you would seek to be like Him more and more (Ephesians 5:1-2).

Prayer for Personal Needs

Now that you've confessed your sin and focused on God's character, you are ready to petition Him for your own needs. In this, you open your heart to God and express your concerns, needs, desires and plans. In doing so, you acknowledge your dependence upon Him for all things.

Spiritual growth
- Sensitivity to sin
- Greater love and commitment to the Lord

Need for Wisdom
- Wisdom for living life
- Developing an eternal perspective
- Renewal of my mind
- Understanding and searching Scripture

Relationships with Others
- Greater love and compassion for lost; loved ones
- That I would be a good model

Faithfulness as a steward
- With my time
- With my talents
- With my treasures

Pray Psalm 25:16-21 to God.

Prayer for Others

The time has come to focus on others needs and your involvement with them. Seven areas will be considered:

The church and other ministries
- My local church
- Other churches
- Other Christian ministries
- My denomination

Family
- My immediate family
- Relatives
- Salvation; growth

Believers
- Personal friends
- People in ministry
- Those oppressed around the world

Evangelism
- Friends
- Family
- Associates

Government
- Local/State
- National
- Elections

Missions
- Local/national
- World
- Fulfillment of the Great Commission

World Affairs
- Poor and hungry
- Oppressed and persecuted
- Those in authority

Prayers of Thanksgiving
This time of prayer expresses gratitude for who God is and what He has done. It's an important ingredient in prayer because it causes you to reflect upon and remember God's work in your life. This, in turn, increases your confidence in the way He will continue to work.

Count your blessings
- salvation
- health
- material blessings

- friends
- answered prayer
- family
- country
- sovereignty

How To Spend An Hour With God – 5

Scripture Reading: The book of Philippians

Prayers of Adoration

1 Chronicles 29:10-13:

Blessed are you, LORD God of Israel,
    our Father, forever and ever.
Yours, O LORD, is the greatness, The power and the glory,
    For all that is in heaven and in earth is Yours;
Yours is the kingdom, O LORD,
    And You are exalted as head over all.
Both riches and honor come from You,
    And You reign over all.
In Your hand it is to make great
    And to give strength to all.
Now therefore, our God, We thank You
    And praise Your glorious name.

Prayers for Forgiveness

Psalm 103:8-14:

You are merciful and gracious,
    Slow to anger, and abounding in mercy.
You will not always strive with us,
    Nor will you keep Your anger forever.
You have not dealt with us according to our sins,
    Nor punished us according to our iniquities.
For as the heavens are high above the earth,
    So great is your mercy toward those who fear You;
As far as the east is from the west,
    So far have You removed our transgressions from us.
As a father pities his children
    So the Lord pities those who fear Him.
For You know our frame;
You remember that we are dust.

Prayers for Renewal

1 Peter 3:15:

> May I sanctify Christ as Lord in my heart, and always be ready to give a defense to everyone who asks me a reason for the hope that is in me, with meekness and fear.

Colossians 4:5, 6:

> Grant that I may walk in wisdom toward those who are outside, redeeming the time. May my speech always be with grace, seasoned with salt, that I may know how I ought to answer each one.

Hebrews 12:1, 2:

> May I lay aside every weight, and the sin which so easily ensnares me, and may I run with endurance the race that is set before me, looking unto Jesus, the author and finisher of my faith, who for the joy that was set before Him endured the cross, despising the shame, and has sat down at the right hand of the throne of God.

Pause here for any additional prayers for renewal.

Prayers for Personal Needs

Spiritual Insight:

- Who I am
- Why I am here
- Understanding and insight into the Word
- Where I came from
- Where I am going
- Understanding my identity in Christ
- The leading of the Lord and insight into God's will
- Special concerns
- My activities for this day

Prayer for Others

Believers:

- Personal friends
- People in ministry
- Those around the world who are oppressed and in need
- Special concerns

Prayers of Affirmation

2 Corinthians 4:6, 7:

> For it is the God who commanded light to shine out of darkness, who has shone in our hearts to give the light of the knowledge of the glory of God in the face of Jesus Christ. But we have this treasure in earthen vessels, that the excellence of the power may be of God and not of us.

Pause here to add any personal affirmations.

Prayers of Thanksgiving

1 Samuel 2:1, 2:

> My heart rejoices in the LORD;
>> My horn is exalted in the LORD.
> I smile at my enemies,
>> Because I rejoice in Your salvation.
> No one is holy like the LORD,
>> For there is none besides You,
> Nor is there any rock like our God.

Psalm 46:1

> God is our refuge and strength,
> A very present help in trouble.

Hebrews 13:15:

> Therefore by Him let us continually offer the sacrifice of praise to God, that is, the fruit of our lips, giving thanks to His name.

Pause here for any personal expressions of thanksgiving.

Closing Prayers

Numbers 6:24-26:

> The LORD bless you
> and keep you;
> The LORD make His face shine upon you,
> and be gracious to you;
> The LORD lift up His countenance upon you,
> and give you peace.

Romans 15:13:

> Now may the God of hope fill us with all joy and peace
> in believing, that we may abound in hope by the power of
> the Holy Spirit.

Memorize a verse of Scripture you need for your life.

Chapter 7

Personal Life Mission

READY. AIM. FIRE! I am thinking that most people know this line but very few follow its wisdom. Most of us live more like, READY. FIRE. AIM! The latter is a difficult life to live. Once the bullet is out of the gun, it's on a path. There is a momentum that drives that bullet to its target.

I work with people for a living. Most of them want to get to the same destination. But very few people actually take the time to map out their lives. They spend a lot of time on what will not last for eternity. They have a great grasp on their portfolio. They work diligently on their mission statement for the place that employs them. But very few people work hard at the one thing that is an absolute. One day, each of us will stand before our Maker and give an account of our lives. There are only two things that last forever: The Word of God and people. I suggest we spend some time mapping out a personal mission statement that will invest in God's eternal portfolio. We need to ask ourselves, "Do I have a personal mission statement? What do I live my life for? Whom do I live my life for? What will the legacy of my life be?"

Am I on the Critical P.A.T.H?

Path is a word that speaks of direction. We are all on a path leading somewhere. We all hope we are on the right path. Four great "characters" journey down this path together each day. As they rise early in the morning and exercise and give themselves to this daily discipline, they find themselves healthier today than they were yesterday.

What are the names of those characters? They are Passion, Attitude, Thanksgiving and Honor. These characters speak well for themselves. They are words that ought to be included in all our personal mission statements. Anyone can follow a path, but only a leader can blaze one. When we are ready to take the journey of life and live out our purpose, we should know there might be a lot of people who are depending upon us. We choose to give our time and resources to the things that are important to us.

Family and friends need people who model purpose-driven lives. It has been said, "If you aim at nothing, you will hit it every time." What is it that we are passionately pursuing?

Children need parents who help them reach their potential. It has been said, "our potential is God's gift to us and what we do with it is our gift to Him." Many people never really dedicate themselves to their purpose in life. They become a jack-of-all-trades and a master-of-none rather than a jack of few trades, focused on one. Investing our time in our children and teaching them godly values is a paramount purpose for life.

Churches need people who chart a course and equip the saints. Balance is everything. I have learned to operate under a simple equation that I believe is the key to successful leadership. It will put a person on the right path! It goes like this: PURPOSE + PROCESS + EXECUTION = SUCCESS.

When we know what our purpose is and when we put together a strategic process that will point us toward our destination, and when we organize a detailed, accountable plan and timeline that maps out the steps that will get us to our destination, then we reach our potential.

Businesses need leaders and workers who build great places to work while making a profit. The business community might say, "Show me the bottom line." I am a bottom line kind of guy!

The heart of the matter is defining the bottom line. Is it money or people? There is nothing wrong if money is in our view, but people must clearly be our focus. An organization exists because of people. They are the most treasured assets. Do I work hard at making the work environment a fun place? Do I work hard at purposefully serving my congregation, customers, or clients?

Communities need people who can create a better place to live. Home is where we hang our hat. Where is our community? Who is our community? Instead of being a typical consumer, why not consider giving something back to the community? With an attitude of thanksgiving and a spirit of honor, consider that we exist in such a community because of the sacrifices of men and women who journeyed down the path before us.

They chose the right path, to live a life of service. Jesus said, *The Son of Man did not come to be served, but to serve, and to give his life as a ransom for many* (Matthew 20:28). He also said, *Whoever wants to become great among you must be your servant, and whoever wants to be first must be slave of all* (Mark 10:43–44). If we want to be great, we have to be a servant of all.

If I will just take a few minutes every day to make sure I am following the ultimate leader and learn His leadership lessons, I will undoubtedly blaze a path that takes me— and my people—where only God can lead. As I journey down the right P.A.T.H. I hope it will not be just any path but the one path God has mapped out for my life personally!

If I had to define my life in one word, what word would I use? Would I say, "Hectic"? "Busy"? "Fun"? Would I think to use the word "Purposeful"? With a purpose, a life mission, each day is special. Is my life mission central to my thinking when I wake up each morning?

Jesus had a life mission. We read what He said in John 17:4, *I have brought you glory on earth by completing the work you gave me to do.* I'd like to be able to say that about my life mission. The purpose of man is to bring glory to God. But how do I do that?

I bring glory to God by fulfilling my purpose. I bring glory to God by completing the work He gives me to do—a work that is unique to me. Nobody else can do it; it is my life mission.

What Is a Life Mission?

A life mission is what I believe God wants me to do with my life. It's an explanation of who I am and what I have been put here on earth to do. A life mission is more than a goal. Many people confuse their goal with their life mission. Goals are worthless unless we have an over-arching life mission, to know what brings everything about us into focus.

Our mission is based on God's purpose for us. Our life mission is really the reason we exist. It's why God put each of us on this earth. It expresses the unique design or shape that God created us to be. That life-mission includes everything about us. It will use our own personalities, our experiences, our spiritual gifts, our heart and passion, and our abilities. Our life mission will fully express who we are.

One way to discover our purpose for life is through the user manual of our Creator—the Bible. God tells us what He wants us to do with our lives. *Don't act thoughtlessly, but try to understand what the Lord wants you to do* (Ephesians 5:17 NLT).

No one can tell another person what his or her specific mission in life is. We don't know it. Each of us has to discover his own life mission over time. It's a process, not simply a one-shot deal.

Discovering Our Life Mission

What questions do we need to ask if we are serious about discovering our life mission? Our lives are worth spending purposeful time thinking about it. Is the rest of life important enough for a person to say, "I ought to plan it. I ought to look at my life to see what I'm going to do with the rest of it, what God wants me to do with my life"?

First we need to determine what will be the center of my life? Who or what am I going to live for? We have to start with this. We must have something at the center of our lives around which everything else is built. There are many options. We could center our lives on building a career or our family or making money or pleasure or maybe even becoming popular. None of these things is really going to last. God made us to center our lives on Him. The apostle Paul said, *Everything else is worthless when compared with the priceless gain of knowing Christ Jesus my Lord. I have discarded everything else, counting it all as garbage, so that I may have Christ* (Philippians 3:8 NLT). Each of us has to ask, "Do I know God or do I just know about Him?"

Next, I have to consider what will be the character of my life? What kind of person am I going to be? God is far more interested in who I am than in what I do. Scripture says that God made us to become like Christ. *God knew what he was doing from the very beginning. He decided from the outset to shape the lives of those who love him along the same lines as the life of his Son. The Son stands first in the line of humanity he restored. We see the original and intended shape of our lives there in him* (Romans 8:29 MsgB).

God wants me to learn to think like Jesus, to talk like Jesus, to act like Jesus. What does that mean? *But the fruit of the Spirit is love, joy, peace, patience, kindness, goodness, faithfulness, gentleness and self-control* (Galatians 5:22–23). God wants to build those nine qualities in my life and in the life of every believer. He wants to make us loving, joyful, peaceful—all those qualities.

Then I have to think about the contribution of my life. What will that contribution be? What am I going to give back to God and to others? What am I going to do with my God-given talents? I wasn't put here on earth just to take; I was put here to give. I was put here to make a contribution with my life, to put something into this world that will make it a better place. *God has given gifts to each of you from his great variety of spiritual gifts. Manage them well so that God's generosity can flow through you* (1 Peter 4:10 NLT).

It is God Himself who has made us what we are and has given us new lives in Christ Jesus. Long ago He planned that we should spend these lives in helping others.

Two Types of People

There are two types of people in life: those who give and those who take. I can live my life selfishly or I can live my life unselfishly. I may make a living by what I get, but I make a life by what I give. Nobody is ever remembered by what he or she got out of life. Abundant living comes from abundant giving. Life is a test. God is testing how much we give, our generosity on this earth. Jesus told those who were faithful in a few things that He would entrust them with many things.

I need to think through the question, "What will be the communication of my life?" What will be my life message? God wants to say something to the world and He has chosen to say it through you and me. That message is given through our words and our actions. He made us to tell others about Him. If I don't tell the people He has placed in my life about Him, then how are they going to know? How would I have known if somebody hadn't told me? God wants us all to share Christ with others. The Bible says, *We are ambassadors for Christ* (2 Cor. 5:20 NASB). *My life is worth nothing unless I use it for doing the work assigned me by the Lord Jesus—the work of telling others the Good News about God's wonderful kindness and love* (Acts 20:24 NLT).

In Steven Covey's book *Principle-Centered Leadership*, he suggests we write out our life mission by beginning at the end of our life. He says to imagine yourself at your own funeral. Four people in your life—someone from your family, your church, your career, and a friend—stand up to talk about you. What would you like them to say about you at the end of your life? Then Covey says to go back and write out a life message based on what you want them to say about you. What Covey is teaching is good, but it's not good enough because what really matters at the end of our lives is not what other people say about us. What matters most is what God is going to say about us. In 2 Corinthians 10:13 (TLB) we read, *Our goal is to measure up to God's plan for us.*

A Mission for Each of Us

God has a mission for each one of us. *The most important thing is that I complete my mission, the work that the Lord Jesus gave me—to tell people the Good News about God's grace* (Acts 20:24 NCV). When we carry out that mission it brings glory to God! *I have brought you glory on earth by completing the work you gave me to do* (Jesus, John 17:4).

God, in creating us, prepared us with a personal mission, a local mission, and a global mission. That mission is the same for every believer: *You are to go into all the world and preach the Good News to everyone, everywhere* (Mark 16:15, TLB). *"You must warn them so they may live. If you don't speak out to warn the wicked to stop their evil ways, they will die in their sin. But I will hold you responsible for their death* (Ezek. 3:18, NCV). *Telling the Good News is my duty—something I must do. And how terrible it will be for me if I do not tell the Good News* (1 Cor. 9:16 NCV).

The great 18th century preacher Jonathan Edwards said, "God tells us that he shall look upon what is done in charity to our neighbors in want, as done unto him and what is denied unto them, as denied unto him. 'He that hath pity upon the poor lendeth unto the Lord' (Proverbs 19:7 KJV). God hath been pleased to make our needy neighbors his receivers."[1]

Mother Teresa, who had a mission to the dying in Calcutta, India, said, "We ourselves feel that what we are doing is just a drop in the ocean. But if that drop was not in the ocean, I think

[1] Jonathan Edwards, *Christian Charity or The Duty of Charity to the Poor, Explained and Enforced* (Columbus, N.J.: Bible Bulletin Board).

the ocean would be less because of that missing drop. I do not agree with the big way of doing things."[2]

There is a great question that comes from Luke 10:2. That question is, do we "tend to be what God wants us to be?" *The harvest is plentiful, but the workers are few. Ask the Lord of the Harvest, therefore, to send out workers into his harvest field* (Luke 10:2).

Our mission begins at the personal level. I know I have to develop a top-ten list and begin serving the individuals who walk through life with me. Our mission then expands to the local level. It is here that I engage with other people who are carrying out their mission to do something eternal in the community where God has placed me. Our mission comes full circle when we take it globally. As you and I develop our personal mission, we need to make sure that we paint the picture with the perspective of our Creator. He who loves the world is God!

Following the Heart of Jesus

Our Creator has a big heart. Maybe we don't know where to start serving and sharing this good news. We can start by capturing the heart of Jesus and following His example.

The heart of Jesus is for the hungry, the thirsty, the homeless, the poor, the sick and infirm. He is for the prisoner, the widow, the orphan and the oppressed (Matthew 25:31–46; Luke 4:18–19; James 1:27; Malachi 3:5). This list is a great place to start on our life's mission.

Our life mission should be expressed through Christ, through one another, and through the world. How will we establish our life around an intimate relationship with the King of the Universe, our Creator, our Savior and Friend? How will we serve those who live in our community? And how will we take God's eternal message of Good News to the people of the world who are lost and hopeless? This is the beginning of our

[2] Edward Le Joly and Jaya Chaliha, *Stories Told by Mother Teresa* (Santa Clara,Calif.: Charityfocus.org.)

mission! It is a race. It is a journey. Stay the course; finish your race. The habits you develop in your spiritual fitness program will give you ABS of Faith. You are prepared to cross the finish line and hear the final words of your Heavenly Father: *Well done, good and faithful servant! You have been faithful with a few things; I will put you in charge of many things. Come and share your master's happiness!* (Matthew 25:23).

Use the following tools to assist you in creating your personal mission statement: "A Life on Purpose—Personal Planner" and "S.H.A.P.E. Profile Worksheet." They will help you find the unique fit and shape for which God created you.

Spend your time and energy in training yourself for spiritual fitness (1 Timothy 4:7 NLT).

A Life On Purpose
Personal Planner

Purpose *Primary Questions* • Suggested Topics	Plans *Specific, measurable, & realistic*
Community (Fellowship) *How can I deepen my relationships with God's Family?* • Small Group Community • Family/Friends • Spiritual Mentors	• cultivate greater relational intimacy • honor time with my family & friends • identify a personal mentor
Maturity (Discipleship) *How can I grow in my spiritual journey with Christ?* • Prayer and Bible Study • Personal Devotions/Quiet Time • Spiritual Disciplines	• begin journaling my prayers • regularly read God's Word • develop personal budget for the new year
Ministry (Service) *How can I further discover and develop my God-given S.H.A.P.E?* • Ministry Opportunities • Vocational Developments • Continuing Education/Training	• read small group leaders book • attend ministry class • explore a new ministry area • take a Bible class in college
Missions (Evangelism) *How can I share Christ with others and fulfill my life's mission?* • Work/Neighborhood Activities • Personal Evangelism • Cross-Cultural Involvement	• start monthly lunch with seeker friends • pray for my non-believing relatives • sponsor an orphan child in another country
Surrender (Worship) *How can I grow in my personal and corporate worship of God?* • Regular Church Attendance • Worship Tapes & Devotionals • Personal Health & Balance	• attend services with my group • purchase a worship tape/CD for my car • regular exercise and nutrition • seek balance in my life

S.H.A.P.E. Profile Worksheet

(to help discover or develop your God-given S.H.A.PE.)

Spiritual Gifts
- ☐ Preaching (1 Corinthians 14:3)
- ☐ Evangelism (Acts 8:26–40)
- ☐ Discernment (1 John 4:1)
- ☐ Apostle (Romans 15:20)
- ☐ Teaching (Ephesians 4:12–13)
- ☐ Encouragement (Acts 14:22)
- ☐ Wisdom (1 Corinthians 2:1, 6–16)
- ☐ Missions (1 Corinthians 9:19–23, Acts 13:2-3)
- ☐ Service (Acts 6:1–7,Corinthians 12:28)
- ☐ Mercy (Romans 12:8)
- ☐ Hospitality (1 Peter 4:9–10)
- ☐ Pastoring (1 Peter 5:2–4)
- ☐ Giving (2 Corinthians 8:1–7)
- ☐ Intercession (Colossians 1:9–12)
- ☐ Music (Psalm 150)
- ☐ Arts & Crafts (Exodus 31:3–11)
- ☐ Healing (James 5:14-16)
- ☐ Miracles (Mark 11:23–24)
- ☐ Leadership (Hebrews 13:7, 17)
- ☐ Administration (1 Corinthians 4:40)
- ☐ Faith (Romans 4:18–21)

Heart - I Love To ...
- ☐ Design/Develop
- ☐ Pioneer
- ☐ Organize
- ☐ Operate/Maintain
- ☐ Serve/Help
- ☐ Acquire/Possess
- ☐ Excel
- ☐ Perform
- ☐ Improve
- ☐ Repair
- ☐ Lead/Be in Charge
- ☐ Persevere
- ☐ Follow the Rules
- ☐ Prevail
- ☐ Influence

Abilities
- ☐ Entertaining
- ☐ Recruiting
- ☐ Interviewing
- ☐ Researching
- ☐ Artistic/Graphics
- ☐ Evaluating
- ☐ Planning
- ☐ Managing
- ☐ Counseling
- ☐ Teaching
- ☐ Writing/Editing
- ☐ Promoting
- ☐ Repairing
- ☐ Feeding
- ☐ Recall
- ☐ Mechanical/Operating
- ☐ Resourceful
- ☐ Counting/Classifying
- ☐ Public Relations
- ☐ Welcoming
- ☐ Composing
- ☐ Landscaping
- ☐ Arts & Crafts
- ☐ Decorating
- ☐ Musical

Personality
Extroverted ☐ ☐ ☐ Introverted
Routine ☐ ☐ ☐ Variety
Self-Control ☐ ☐ ☐ Self-Expressive
Cooperative ☐ ☐ ☐ Competitive

Experiences
- ☐ Spiritual
- ☐ Painful
- ☐ Educational
- ☐ Vocational
- ☐ Ministry

Additional Resources

How to Have a Quiet Time

Christian Growth
Bible Study

Nothing is of greater importance for Christian growth than the habit of a daily time in Bible reading, meditation, and prayer. This study has been designed to guide you into a life of close fellowship with God. Look up each verse; then prayerfully write down the answer to the question in your own words.

What is a Quiet Time?
It is a time of worship, devotion, and fellowship with God. To what have we been called? 1 Corinthians 1:9

_____

_____

_____

There are 1,440 minutes in each 24-hour day. Up till now, how many minutes have you been setting aside for communion with God?

_____

Why is Quiet Time so important?
First, it takes time to get to know our Father. What was Paul's main prayer? Philippians 3:10

_____

_____

_____

Second, we need a starting point for the day...a time to get our bearings ... to see our nothingness and His all sufficiency! Third, it pleases God and makes Him happy for us to pray to Him. What does God seek from you? John 4:23

_____

_____

_____

When is Quiet Time best?
What time do you usually get up in the morning?

_____

What was Jesus' custom in prayer? Mark 1:35

_____

At night ask God to help you get up in the morning. What are some disadvantages of postponing Quiet Time until the last thing at night?

_____

_____

_____

What time would you have to get up to give God 15 minutes tomorrow morning before you go to work or school?

_____

What did Jesus counsel concerning regular time? Matthew 6:6

_____

_____

_____

Where to pray?
Where can we pray? 1 Timothy 2:8

_____

_____

_____

Many people find it best to walk outside to pray. Others sit in a car, go to an extra room or closet or to other places in the house ... but get alone we must. What place can you think of now where you could have 7–15 minutes with God?

_____

_____

_____

What to do in Quiet Time

Read daily Bible readings, a devotional guide, or Scripture passages. Ask God to speak to you. You want to experience His nearness and presence, to receive orders, warnings, and peace. Then pray.

List what keeps our prayers from being answered:

a. Mark 11:25

_____

_____

b. 1 Peter 3:7

_____

_____

c. James 4:3

_____

_____

d. Psalm 66:18

_____

_____

e. Proverbs 28:9

_____

_____

How must we prepare for successful praying? 1 John 1:9

_____

_____

How to apply Scripture
First ask: What did it mean to the original hearers?
Second ask: What is the underlying timeless principle?
Third ask: Where or how could I practice that principle?

Remember
When plain sense makes common sense, seek no other sense.
Let the Spirit of God be your teacher and guide.

Heart-Searching for

Prayer, Preparation, and Personal Revival

"**S**earch me, O God, and know my heart: try me, and know my thoughts: And see if there be any wicked way in me, and lead me in the way everlasting" (Psalm 139:23–24 KJV).

Confession of sin is necessary for fellowship with God and revival among God's people. Prayerfully consider the following questions. Answer them truthfully one by one. A yes answer indicates there is sin in your life.

In reading these questions, as you are convicted of sin, confess it at once to God. Be willing to make it right. Then you can claim cleansing and forgiveness. "If we confess our sins, he is faithful and just to forgive us our sins, and to cleanse us from all unrighteousness" (1 John 1:9 KJV).

Be sure to name your sin to God, as: "Lord, I have not put you first in my plans," or "I have neglected Your Word and prayer." Do not make the least excuse for sin of any kind in your life. "He that covereth his sins shall not prosper: but whoso confesseth and forsaketh them shall have mercy" (Proverbs 28:13 KJV).

No matter what others do or do not do, Christian, leave nothing undone on your part. God wants to work through you to bring about a great spiritual awakening. He can begin by your fulfilling every requirement shown by the Lord through the Holy Spirit and His Word. A revival from the presence of the Lord begins today—if you desire it! (Read the Scriptures first. Ask the question. Give a truthful answer—yes or no.)

1. **Matthew 6:12–14**—Is there anyone against whom you hold a grudge? Anyone you haven't forgiven? Anyone you hate? Anyone you do not love? Are there any misunderstandings you are unwilling to forget? Is there any person against whom you are harboring bitterness, resentment, or jealousy? Anyone you dislike to hear praised or well spoken of? Do you allow anything to justify a wrong attitude toward another?

2. **Matthew 6:33**—Is there anything in which you have failed to put God first? Have your decisions been made after your own wisdom and desires, rather than seeking and following God's will? Do any of the following in any way interfere with your surrender and service to God: ambition, pleasures, loved ones, friendships, desire for recognition, money, your own plans?

3. **Mark 16:15**—Have you failed to seek the lost for Christ? Have you failed to witness consistently with your mouth for the Lord Jesus Christ? Has your life not shown the Lord Jesus to the lost?

4. **John 13:35**—Are you secretly pleased over the misfortunes of another? Are you secretly annoyed over the accomplishments or advancements of another? Are you guilty of any contention or strife? Do you quarrel, argue or engage in heated discussions? Are you a partaker in any divisions or party spirit? Are there people whom you deliberately slight? Does your attitude reflect the "love" of Jesus as you respond to others?

5. **Acts 20:35; Malachi 3:8**—Have you robbed God by withholding His due of time, talents and money? Have you given less than a tenth of your income for God's work? Have you failed to support missions, either in prayer or in offering?

6. **1 Corinthians 4:2**—Are you undependable so you cannot be trusted with responsibilities in the Lord's work? Are you allowing your emotions to be stirred for things of the Lord but doing nothing about it?

7. **1 Corinthians 6:19–20**—Are you in any way careless with your body? Do you fail to care for it as the temple of the Holy Spirit? Are you guilty of intemperance in eating or drinking? Do you have any habits that are defiling to the body?

8. **1 Corinthians 10:31**—Do you take the slightest credit for anything good about you, rather than giving all the glory to God? Do you talk of what you have done rather than what Christ has done? Are your statements full of "I"? Are your feelings easily hurt? Have you made a pretense of being something you are not?

9. **Ephesians 3:20**—Are you self-conscious rather than Christ-conscious? Do you allow feelings of inferiority to keep you from attempting things you should in serving God?

10. **Ephesians 4:28**—Do you underpay? Do you do very little in your work? Have you been careless in the payment of your debts? Have you sought to evade payment of debts? Do you waste time? Do you waste time for others?

11. **Ephesians 4:31**—Do you complain? Do you find fault? Do you have a critical attitude toward any person or thing? Are you irritable or cranky? Do you ever carry hidden anger? Do you get angry? Do you become impatient with others? Are you ever harsh or unkind?

12. **Ephesians 5:16; Philippians 4:4**—Do you listen to unedifying radio or watch unwholesome TV programs or visit unhealthy web sites? Do you read unworthy magazines? Do you partake in worldly amusements? Do you find it necessary to seek satisfaction from any questionable source? Are you doing certain things that show you are not satisfied in the Lord Jesus Christ?

13. **Ephesians 5:20**—Have you neglected to thank Him for all things, the seemingly bad as well as the good? Have you virtually called God a liar by doubting His Word? Do you worry? Is your spiritual temperature based on your feelings instead of on the facts of God's Word?

14. **Philippians 1:21**—Are you taken up with the cares of this life? Is your conversation or heart joy over "things" rather than the Lord and His Word? Does anything mean more to you than living for and pleasing Christ?

15. **Philippians 2:14**—Do you ever by word or deed seek to hurt someone? Do you gossip? Do you speak unkindly concerning people when they are not present? Do you carry prejudice against true Christians because they are of some different group than yours, or because they do not see everything exactly as you do?

16. **Philippians 4:4**—Have you neglected to seek to be pleasing to Him in all things? Do you carry any bitterness toward God? Have you complained against Him in any way? Have you been dissatisfied with His provision for you? Is there in your heart any unwillingness to obey God fully? Do you have any reservations as to what you would or would not do concerning anything that might be His will? Have you disobeyed some direct leading from Him?

17. **Colossians 3:9**—Do you engage in empty and unprofitable conversation? Do you ever lie? Do you ever exaggerate? Cheat? Steal? Carefully consider—do you overcharge?

18. **2 Timothy 2:22**—Do you have any personal habits that are not pure? Do you allow impure thoughts about the opposite sex to stay in your mind? Do you read what is impure or suggests unholy things? Do you indulge in any unclean entertainment? Are you guilty of the lustful look?

19. **Hebrews 10:25**—Do you stay away from the meetings of preaching the gospel? Do you whisper or think about other things while God's Word is being read or preached? Are you irregular in attendance at services? Do you neglect to attend or participate in meetings for prayer? Have you neglected or slighted daily or private prayer? Have you neglected God's Word? Do you find the Bible and prayer uninteresting? Have you neglected thanksgiving at meals? Have you neglected daily family devotions?

20. **Hebrews 13:17**—Do you hesitate to submit to leaders in the church or elsewhere? Are you lazy? Do you rebel at requests given to you to help in the work of the gospel? Do you in any way have a stubborn or unreachable spirit?

21. **James 1:27**—Has your journey with Christ become all about you? Do you look at your world with eyes like Jesus? What are you doing for the social injustices in our world today? Are you helping the widows, the orphans, and the poor in our world?

22. **James 4:6**—Do you feel that you are doing quite well as a Christian? That you are not so bad? That you are good enough? Are you stubborn? Do you insist on having your own way? Do you insist on your rights?

23. **James 4:11**—Have you dishonored God and hindered His work by criticizing His servants? Have you failed to pray regularly for your pastor or other spiritual leaders? Do you find it hard to be corrected? Is there rebellion toward one who wants to restore you? Are you more concerned about what people will think than what will be pleasing to God?

If you have been honest and true in the matter of admitting your sins, you are ready for God's cleansing. Sins that are admitted are sins that are confessed. Remember these three things:

1. If the sin is against God, confess it to God and make things right with God.

2. If the sin is against another person, confess it to God and make things right with the other person.

3. If the sin is against a group, confess it to God and make it right with the group.

If there is full confession, there will be full cleansing. Then the joy of the Lord will follow. Then there can be testimony and prayer in the power of the Holy Spirit. Revival will follow.

"Who can understand his errors? Cleanse thou me from secret faults" (Psalm 19:12 KJV).

How to Deal with

Temptation

What Is Temptation?

(James l:13-15)

1. The reality of temptation (v.13). James says *when* you are tempted, not *if* you are tempted.

2. The source of temptation (v.13)
    - God is not the source.
    - There are three sources:
      o World's system (1 John 2:15–16)
      o Satan (Matthew 4:3)
      o Sin nature (James l:13–14)
    - The process of temptation (vv.14–15)
      o We are enticed by evil.
      o Our desires are attracted.
      o We give in and sin.
      o We pay the consequences.

God's Promise Concerning Temptation

1. God has put a limit on the power of temptation (1 Corinthians 10:13).

2. God has made an escape route for every temptation (1 Corinthians 10:13).
   - God does not remove temptation (John 17:15).
   - God knows how to rescue us (2 Peter 2:9).

Christ's Advice About Temptation

(Matthew 26:41)

1. Be alert to temptation. Keep your eyes open.

2. Pray about temptation.

Christ's Example in Temptation

(Matthew 4:1–11)

1. Christ had the Bible memorized.

2. Christ quoted the Bible outloud.

3. Christ used Scripture that related to His temptation.

4. Six ways to use the Bible in temptation:
   - Memorize it (Psalm 119:11).
   - Learn its teachings (Psalm 119:12).
   - Recite it outloud (Psalm 119:13).
   - Obey it (Psalm 119:14).
   - Think about it (Psalm 119:15).
   - Give it priority (Psalm 119:16).

Personal Journal

Journaling is not for everyone, but it is a good tool to use when God speaks to you and/or reveals something to you as you read the Bible or meditate on what you are learning or when you are challenged by a message. Use this page to record your thoughts. You don't have to write a book, but write what God is impressing on your heart. There is no better way to remember important truths that God is revealing to you. Save them and review your thoughts at the end of each month. Include today's date, the passage you are reading, and your response in written prayers to God.

_____

_____

_____

_____

_____

_____

_____

_____

_____

_____

_____

_____

_____

_____

_____

_____

_____

_____

"Before we disciple others, we ourselves must learn what it takes to be a disciple. A disciple will always take time to sit at the feet of Jesus"
— *Greg Laurie.*

Personal Testimony Worksheet

Preparing your story to be shared with friends and family

Key Principles

- Be specific, be realistic, and be positive.
- Develop your testimony so you can simply and cleverly share it in three minutes or less.
- Practice sharing it in your small group.
- Commit to sharing with one or two seeker friends in the next 30 days.

1. Before I received Christ (*I lived and thought this way…*)

_____

_____

_____

_____

_____

2. How I received Christ *(describe the process leading to your decision)*

_____

_____

_____

_____

_____

3. After I received Christ *(how I trust, live, and seek to please God with my life)*

_____

_____

_____

_____

_____

ABS Abstractions

Accountability
Bible Reading
Scripture Memory

Although there are spiritual disciplines toward which we must work, there is also an abstract reality of responsibility that defines the essence of the discipline.

Although we need to be accountable, you are truly the *only* one who can hold yourself accountable. You have the ability to lie, rationalize, or blow it off.

Although we can read, memorize its words, and learn the truths of the Bible, we can do so and never put it into practice. We are quite capable of "quenching" what the Spirit of God might reveal. When sin "abounds" in our lives, we might not clearly hear what God says to us. We must guard against reading and memorizing for informational purposes only and put into practice the scriptural truths that are intended to bring change and transform us.

Although relationship with Jesus is reality, there is a colossally more important truth. What Jesus demands is far more than mere relationship. It is an understanding that He is the vine and we are the branches. He is the source of everything. There is a spiritual umbilical cord that connects us to Him. We are totally dependent on Him. We have no life apart from Him. A relationship alone does not cut it.

Although I am alive in Christ, there is a constant need for PRUNING. Pruning is not cutting away just the dead; it is cutting away even what is alive so we might bear more fruit. It is not a once-for-all pruning. At a minimum, pruning should take place regularly, at least annually. Are we creating margin in our lives for God to continue to work through us? Too often our lives are so busy with good that we have left no room for what is best. Is your plate too full? If you have no time left at the end of the day for God, then you are too busy. You are the only person who can say yes or no to what fills up your life. You need some margin!

Your body is the temple of the Holy Spirit. As you build ABS of Faith, are you working equally as hard to take care of your body? "Abs of Steel" might be nice too!

I wish you well as you develop "abs of Steel" but more importantly *ABS of Faith*!

Get Healthy as You Pursue

authentic

SPIRITUAL FITNESS

Go to www.ABSofFaith.com

Engaging resources for you, your church,
your small group and your ABS group!

Here you will find book order discounts and free:

➡ ABS Partner and
   Small Group Resources
➡ Sermons
➡ and More